Challenge Workouts for Advanced Swimmers

DEDICATION
To Lorna Anderson
who believed in me, and my swimming.
She was my biggest fan.

CHALLENGE WORKOUTS

FOR ADVANCED SWIMMERS

by Blythe Lucero

Meyer & Meyer Sport

British Library Cataloguing in Publication Data
A catalogue record for this book is available from the British Library

Challenge Workouts for Advanced Swimmers
Maidenhead: Meyer & Meyer Sport (UK) Ltd., 2010
ISBN 978-1-84126-293-2

© 2010 by Meyer & Meyer Sport (UK) Ltd.
Aachen, Adelaide, Auckland, Budapest, Cape Town, Graz, Indianapolis,
Maidenhead, Olten (CH), Singapore, Toronto
Member of the World
Sport Publishers' Association (WSPA)
www.w-s-p-a.org
Printed by: B.O.S.S Druck und Medien GmbH
ISBN: 978-1-84126-293-2
E-Mail: info@m-m-sports.com
www.m-m-sports.com

TABLE OF CONTENTS

INTRODUCTION 7

GETTING THESE MOST OUT OF THIS BOOK 11
   What is an Advanced Swimmer? . . . .
   Are these Workouts for You? 11
      Swim Level Test 12
      Scoring the Test 13

ADVANCED TRAINING 15
   The Training Needs of Developed Athletes 15
      Begin with Self-Knowledge 18
      Self-Awareness Exercise. 18
   Taking the Challenge 19
      Goal Affirmation 20
      Positive Self-Talk 20
      Focusing on the Task at Hand 20
      Controlling and Adapting. 21
      Visualizing Optimal Performance 21

GETTING STARTED 23
   Routine 23
   Equipment 24
   Workout Shorthand 24
   Workout Presentation 26
   Drills with a Purpose 27

CHALLENGE WORKOUTS 45
   Base/Freestyle Workouts 46
   I.M./Stroke Specialty Workouts 74
   Sprint Workouts 102
   Distance Workouts 130

CONCLUSION 159

CREDITS 159

COLORADO

INTRODUCTION

I remember one Saturday afternoon, when I was 15, my best friend Zonnie invited me to go to Recreational Swim at the pool. The pool was a familiar place to us. It was where we spent an important part of our day, six days a week, as members of the swim team. We were both developed swimmers with dreams of becoming the best. Zonnie was a gifted sprinter. I was the distance swimmer and a true workout monster.

Dedicated to our training routine, we were motivated by the swimmers we had become. Our desire and determination to be great had led us to develop the workout capacity that others envied. We had full body strength that enabled uncanny speed on demand. We had refined swimming technique that allowed thousands of repetitive motions without failure. Being a swimmer was central to our identity. Looking back, we possessed amazing confidence.

So, that Saturday, on a rare weekend that there was no swim meet, Zonnie and I went to the place we knew best. I had never been to Recreational Swim, but if it meant being at the pool, I was ready. Upon arrival, Zonnie immediately went to talk to one of the lifeguards she had a crush on. I sat down on the edge of the pool where I usually did before workout, ready to lead Lane 3. It was rare to see the pool without lane lines, and with dozens of kids splashing through the water in all directions. The air was full of the exuberant squeals and balls flying between friends.

I put my cap on, hopped in the pool and immediately began stroking, as I did every time I got in, to warm up for workout. Within four strokes, I stopped suddenly to avoid a young boy bobbing up and down towards his encouraging father. I cleared my goggles and began swimming again. I hadn't made it ten yards before I swerved to avoid two teenagers playing tag across my path. I stood up again and looked around me. There was no swimming going on at all! People were playing.

At that moment it occurred to me, as I observed the erratic though joyful goings on in the pool, that I had forgotten how to play in the water. Feeling awkward, I proceeded forward doing heads up breaststroke, to prevent any further close encounters, toward the far side of the pool. As I moved at quarter speed, I felt a strange sort of loss. I wondered how, and when, without my awareness, my transformation into a swimming machine had happened.

For quite a while after that Saturday Recreational Swim, I thought about those people playing at the pool, and how I had found myself feeling like a fish out of water in that situation. It bothered me that I could feel so out of my element, in my element. I remember asking myself as I conquered yard after yard, day after day, if being a high level competitive swimmer came at the expense of having fun in the water.

One day, during a high-volume training phase, in preparation for our Winter Championship, the swimmers in my lane were coming into the wall on their final effort in a set of 10 x 200 on a ridiculous interval. I looked around at my teammates who were as red faced and spent as I was. They were smiling, congratulating each other, and exuding pride in their accomplishment. Zonnie was the last to touch the wall. Without missing a heart beat, she cracked a joke about what bringing up the rear did for a sprinter's pride, and a hoot of community laughter filled the air.

Then it all made sense. I was having fun in the pool! I realized that day, that as a developed swimmer, my relationship with the water was different than most other people. To swimmers like me, it is fun to swim hard. It is fun to train for hours on end. Ultimately, I realized that day that I fuel my motivation, and kindle my drive with challenge because it is fun to be a fast swimmer.

This is the third in a three-book series, called "Coach Blythe's Swim Workouts." This book contains challenging workouts for advanced-level training. The first book in the series contains technique-based workouts, designed to help swimmers improve swimming efficiency by focusing on swimming mechanics. The second book contains conditioning workouts, designed to build swimming capacity and versatility. Swimmers may use the material in this book to train for competitive swimming or triathlon on their own, when their coach is not present. These books can also be useful to coaches looking for workout content to use in the training programs they design for their swimmers.

Without the intent of discouraging anyone taking up the wonderful sport of swimming, this book is neither a Learn to Swim manual, nor a Swimming Technique guide. Users of this book are expected to have the ability to move safely through the water, have a solid understanding, both in theory and practice of swimming mechanics, and, have the fitness development to perform these workouts at a certain speed and rate. On page 12, a test is included to evaluate if these workouts are appropriate for you. Always consult a doctor before beginning a fitness routine such as this.

The 100 workouts in this book provide challenging physical and mental workout content for advanced swimmers who have the fitness, maturity, motivation and guts to dedicate to their swimming. The workouts range from 4,000 to 6,000 yards/meters. Specific workouts are included for Base/Freestyle, IM/Stroke Specialty, Sprint, and Distance Swimming. Each workout is designed as a balanced practice session unto itself, but also as a part of a long-term program of training.

So, if you are up for the challenge ... Ready, go!

GETTING THE MOST OUT OF THIS BOOK

What is An Advanced Swimmer?

The workouts and challenges in this book are geared for advanced swimmers. An advanced swimmer can be defined as a swimmer with well developed stroke mechanics, swimming endurance and power. The combination of these elements enables the swimmer to be energy efficient, and use less effort to get across the pool, so more energy remains to swim farther and faster. Efficiency gives a swimmer more training capacity, and more potential for speed.

Advanced swimmers move through the water with less drag; they access more available power; they feel the water better because they have well developed swimming technique. Solid technique is essential essential when doing a high volume training, as the repetitive nature of swimming makes even a small stroke flaw a source of potential injury when it is repeated over and over. Further, advanced swimmers are able to keep going without much decline in quality or speed. The endurance necessary to accomplish high volume workouts, also allows the swimmer to hold a pace. It is also a factor in the swimmer's rate of recovery between sets or repeats. Finally, advanced swimmers have the ability to apply force. This developed strength, or power, gives the advanced swimmer the ability to swim with intensity, and change speeds on demand. Together with well developed stroke mechanics and endurance, power enables the advanced swimmer to swim fast.

Are These Workouts For You?

The benefit from these workouts, is not just in completing them, but in maintaining quality and efficiency throughout each practice session. The level of swimming asked for in these workouts requires well developed technique, endurance and power that enables the athlete to use a base interval of 1:30 for 100 yards/meters freestyle. This interval includes swim time and rest time of at least 15 seconds, that can be maintained for a series of 10 x 100. This rate of 3,000 yards/meters per hour, includes breaks between sets, as well as rests within sets. If the breaks and rests that are designed into each workout are skipped or shortened, in order to keep up, the swimmer will be constantly swimming in a state of fatigue, losing quality, efficiency and speed. Working out in a constant state of fatigue only trains a swimmer to swim slowly for a long time. This is not the goal of this workout collection. Therefore, swimming quality, fitness level and rate of speed should be evaluated carefully before doing these workouts.

Swim Level Test

The following test will be helpful in determining if these workouts are appropriate for you. If you are not sure of an answer, rather than guess, swim what is asked in the questions, and find out.

SWIM LEVEL TEST

Circle the answer that best describes your swimming

POINT VALUE ▶	1	2	3	4
1. How long can you swim without stopping?	200 yds	500 yds	1,500 yds	3,000 yds
2. Can far can you swim in an hour?	2,000 yds	2,500 yds	3,000 yds	4,000 yds
3. Do you have shoulder pain when you swim or a shoulder condition?	Yes	Sometimes	I used to	No
4. How many competitive strokes can you swim 100 yds or more?	1 stroke	2 strokes	3 strokes	4 strokes
5. What is your interval for 10 x 100 yds Freestyle?	2:00	1:50	1:40	1:30
6. What is your interval for 5 x 200 yds Freestyle?	4:00	3:30	3:15	3:00

Scoring the Test

If all of your answers are in Column 4:
These workouts are appropriate for you. Proceed to the next section, which describes the philosophy behind theses workouts. If you are a swimmer whose answers could have fallen into Column 5, meaning you have more endurance, technique and speed than is required, don't dismiss these workouts as too easy. Remember, these workouts are an exercise in personal challenge, not represented only by yardage or interval.

If all of your answers are in Column 3:
These workouts will be hard for you. Before deciding to do these workouts, you should spend time making sure your swimming technique is sound, so shoulder problems do not come up again. You should also ask yourself if you are ready to lower your interval on 100s and 200s, as it will be required.

If all of your answers are in Column 1 or 2:
These workouts are not appropriate for you. Consider the other two books in this series, "Technique Swim Workouts" or "Shape Up" workouts. Both books contain excellent workouts which will help you improve your technique, endurance and speed.

If your answers fall under multiple columns:
Assuming no answers are in Column 1, add the point value above the column of each answer you circled. Total your score and use the following guidelines to see if these workouts are for you:

Score over 23   Yes.
Score of 17 – 22 No. Try "Shape Up" Workouts (2nd book of this series)
Score under 17 No. Try "Technique Swim Workouts" (1st book of this series)

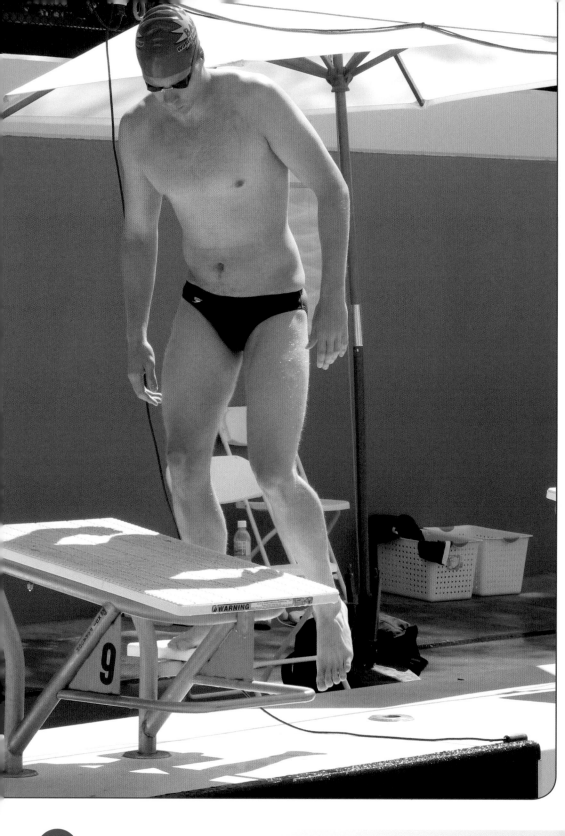

ADVANCED TRAINING

The Training Needs of Developed Athletes

Equipped with superior endurance, refined technique and awesome strength, the workout capacity of developed swimmers is quite extraordinary. This high level of fitness is the result of a lot of time in the water. Its cumulative effect allows these athletes the to train frequently, for long periods of time, at a high rate of speed. There are, however, two unexpected consequences of training with this level of swimming fitness.

1. Swimmers can become so fit that workouts do not phase them. Known as "the more you do, the more you have to do" syndrome, there is a danger of overtraining that can lead to fatigue rather than improvement.

2. In competition, high capacity for training does not always mirror the rate of improvement. In fact, smaller degrees of improvement are often seen as fitness level rises.

In order for these athletes to continue career progress of faster times in competition, their training needs must to be carefully planned.

There are many theories on the correct emphasis of training for developed athletes. One theory outlines a program that focuses on swimming technique. Proponents of this theory point to the undisputed increase in quality swimming after training content in the mechanics of swimming is prioritized early in the development of swimmers. Another theory calls for increased the workout volume. This theory is bolstered by documentation of better times after more and longer training sessions are added during the developmental years of swimmers. Still, another theory suggests that swimming intensity should be the main training emphasis for developed swimmers. This theory sites dramatic improvements seen in developing swimmers when training content demands a higher volume of "race pace" swimming.

While each of these theories has merit, they are all based on successes achieved by swimmers in the early stages of their swimming careers.

The training needs of developed swimmers are different. Still, along with a good strength program and cross training, elements of each of these training models, would contribute to a quality training program for developed athletes, but for different reasons:

Rather than working to establish a foundation of good swimming, technique work should be included to perfect "water handling" skills, including feel for the water, manipulation of water flow and to decrease drag. Rather than building more capacity for work, increased volume should be used in spikes to keep adaptation occurring. Rather than only to sharpen speed, high intensity work should be used to add workload, without volume, again requiring the swimmer to adapt to less familiar work. Even for the most fit athlete the amount of volume and high intensity training must be carefully monitored to avoid training overload and fatigue.

Further, at this stage of swimming, there is another important training component that must be added. In addition to the carefully designed physical training program one of the main priorities must be the training the mind to be ready for competition. Swimmers at this level have the willingness and ability to train physically. They know the feeling of achievement, and their motivation to be better swimmers drives them to train more ... often too much. To meet the needs of athletes of this caliber, the focus of training should be on harnessing the power of their desire, determination and guts, so it can work for them in competition.

The importance of the mental component of performance is underscored here by three great athletes:

"What separates me from my competition is mental toughness."
                                                           – Michael Jordan

"I have won and lost more games with my mind than my physical skills."
                                                           – Tiger Woods

"As fast as I have to."

                                                           – Michael Phelps

(Answering an interviewer at the 2008 Olympics, asking how fast he would swim)

To develop the mental edge recognized by these, and many other great athletes, the training of developed swimmers should integrate mental training into their physical training routine. Both thinking and feeling aspects of the swimmer's mental processes should be addressed, as often both involved, and intertwined in the attitudes and actions that affect performance. The goal is to build athletes who are:

Physically Prepared and Mentally Tough
Mentally Prepared and Physically Tough

This is the main focus of this workout collection. Beyond the physical demand, each workout challenges the swimmer to become actively engaged in developing an array of mental strategies and emotional grounding skills, in order to become better prepared for optimal performance. Swimmers are challenged to tap into their hunger to become champions by using the powerful characteristics that have led them to work so hard in the pool, and applying them to preparing for the mental and emotional pressures of competition. Swimmers will train to build confidence, concentration strategies, positive coping mechanisms and visualization techniques that will equip them to meet their swimming goals.

By involving the swimmer's mind and emotions in the training they will be more ready to perform at their best. We know swimmers are thinking athletes. Yet they are regularly only given the responsibility of coordinating stroke actions, calculating splits, counting laps, and keeping track of times. While these tasks are important, developed swimmers are capable, and in need of more. Their training must incorporate mental and emotional preparation prominently into their physical workout routine, so that in competition, body and mind work together for the athlete.

When we make room for this kind of participation by the advanced swimmer, they can embark on a whole new level of development. It can be motivating, exciting and fun. Most of all, it is empowering, as the swimmer trains feeling that they are becoming more prepared to succeed.

Begin with Self-Knowledge

Before beginning these workouts, spend some time doing the following exercise. Designed to orient you to the mental training to come, the exercise addresses your self-awareness, attitudes and feelings about your swimming in general and about performing in competition.

The exercise consists of a series of questions, which you are to answer. There are no right or wrong answers.

To do this exercise, stand in front of a mirror. You have two tasks:
1. Answer each question out loud, as if you were being interviewed. Be clear and concise, but as descriptive and as detailed as possible.
2. Observe yourself, as if you were watching your interview on television. Watch your facial expressions and body language: Do you appear happy, stressed, indifferent? Notice your tone of voice: Does it sound confident, enthusiastic, discouraged, fatigued? Listen for pauses in your answers: Do they suggest that you haven't thought about the question before, or that you are not sure of your answer? Listen to the answers: Do they paint a complete picture?

Approach this exercise ready to have fun with it. Let your personality come through. Reveal the swimmer that you are.

Self-Awareness Exercise

1. What are your swimming goals for this year? Two years from now?
2. How is swimming fun for you?
3. What strong aspects of your swimming do you want to keep building?
4. What weak aspects of your swimming do you want to improve?
5. When you get tired while training, what do you say to yourself?
6. What distracts you from your swimming goals?

7. What inspires you while you are swimming hard?
8. What makes you doubt yourself?
9. How do you deal with sudden changes in plans?
10. How do you think you look when you are racing?
11. Do you generally do better at home meets or away meets? Why?
12. How did you feel after your biggest swimming achievement?

Having completed your self-interview, you have a lot of food for thought. With each answer you have given, you have had the opportunity to listen to and watch yourself make revealing statements about some of the crucial issues associated with swimming performance. You may have already gained unexpected insight into your personal strengths and weaknesses in terms of your mental and emotional approach to swimming and competing.

Now, as you move through this workout collection and engage in the mental challenges presented, keep your self-interview in mind. This is your starting point. When you have reached the end of the book, do this exercise again, and see how your answers have evolved.

Taking the Challenge

Designed with the training needs of the developed athlete in mind, these workouts have a high degree of difficulty, both physically and mentally. Each workout is goal oriented and flows with the rhyme and reason that will keep training interesting, fun and effective. While many developed swimmers have the capacity to swim longer workouts than the ones contained in this book, remember the challenge goes beyond swimming. These workouts are for thinking swimmers. Done well, the workouts in this book should be the most demanding a swimmer has ever done.

Each workout in this book begins with a personal challenge. It is up to the swimmer to make the most out of that challenge throughout the workout. There are no empty yards in these workouts, not a single one. It is the swimmer's responsibility to demand of him or herself that every stroke counts, every lap is done with purpose and every effort is focused on becoming as prepared mentally and emotionally as the swimmer is prepared physically for competition. Challenges will focus on:

1. Goal Affirmation

Affirming swimming goals underscores the swimmer's commitment to the process of achieving them. Since swimming goals take time and effort to reach, staying committed to them can be challenging at times. Practicing goal affirmation is a way to keep them in focus. Practice is carried out with words, thoughts and actions, including, clearly stating the goal, repeating the goal during tough training sets, identifying with the goal, valuing training as the means to achieve the goal, prioritizing swimming, and showing effort, perseverance and enthusiasm.

2. Positive Self-Talk

The practice of self-talk reflects the swimmer's belief or doubt in his or her abilities. Positive self-talk connects the swimmer's ability to their goal, whereas negative self-talk disconnects the swimmer's ability from their goal. Positive self-talk is a way of building confidence. It involves making positive statements, and actively describing oneself, in the present tense, in terms of having the power, preparation, readiness, talent, skill, and deservedness to achieve the goal. Swimmers can also benefit from developing a vocabulary of personal power words that reinforce their confidence.

3. Focusing on the Task At Hand

The ability to concentrate gives swimmers a real edge in competition, and in training. When a swimmer is able to focus on the task at hand, they are able to channel their energy into the swimming event, or the set that is right in front of them, and give it the full attention it requires to perform at the highest level. With so much going on at swim meets and during workouts, developing concentration strategies and techniques to eliminate distractions, will enable swimmers will be more successful in maintaining and re-gaining the focus they need at crucial times.

4. Controlling and Adapting

Developing the ability to respond positively to unexpected and changing circumstances is an important skill to have. When a swimmer can recognize what they can control, and what they can't, they can avoid being a victim of stressful situations like swim meets, when sleep, eating patterns, weather and schedules can be unpredictable. Swimmers must learn to control what they can, including taking care of themselves and replacing negative thoughts. They must also learn to adapt to what they cannot control by relaxing, building an array of coping strategies and mobilizing under pressure.

5. Visualizing Optimal Performance

Swimmers who practice visualization, are in effect rehearsing the optimal performance of their event. This activity involves developing a mental video that goes through the course of action of the swimmer's event in every detail with the most positive outcome. The swimmer is able to see, hear, feel, smell and taste every aspect of their race physically, mentally and emotionally. Effective visualization includes "rehearsing" the time before, during and after the swim.

GETTING STARTED

To begin this collection of workouts, swimmers should have already taken the Swim Level Test on page 12, and determined that this level of training is appropriate for them. In addition, swimmers should have spent time with the Self-Awareness Exercise on page 18, to orient them to the mental challenges to come.

Next, it is important to develop a routine or training plan. You will also need to collect some equipment, and familiarize yourself with the presentation, terms and drills used throughout these workouts.

Routine

Your swimming routine should be built around competition dates, include work days and rest days, as well as variation in content. Each swimmer's routine may be different, but remember that to maintain the quality and focus that these workouts demand, at least 1-2 rest days per week are recommended.

Whether you are doing base work, or training for freestyle, distance swimming, IM, or sprinting, it is a good idea to build a variety of workouts into your routine. Even when doing stroke specialty training, although most of your training time should be devoted to your stroke specialty, adding some workouts that are different in content accomplishes four important things:

1. **Builds more well-rounded strength through versatility**
2. **Takes the swimmer off "auto pilot"**
3. **Provides rest through variation of work**
4. **Provides a fresh perspective to the swimmer**

Be prepared to modify your routine as the reality of both the physical and mental effects of this training are realized. Remain alert to signs of fatigue. It is important to be sharp every time you practice, in order to make the most of the workout content and challenges presented.

Equipment

The following equipment is called for throughout these workouts:
- **Pace Clock** – or easily visible timing device
- **Pull Buoy** – to be used only when called for. For freestyle pulling only.
- **Fins** – to be used only when called for. Kicking with fins should produce significantly faster times than kicking without fins. If not, they are of no benefit.
- **Kickboard** (Optional) – kicking without a kickboard is preferred, however using a kickboard for Flutter or Breaststroke kick is acceptable and can add variety.

Workout Shorthand

It is important to be familiar with the following terms and swimming jargon used throughout this collection of workouts, appearing here in alphabetical order:

- **100 Easy:** A short recovery swim and a chance to reflect on the set that you just finished
- **25, 50, 75, 100, 200:** Refers to the distance to be done in terms of a 25 yard/meter pool. A 25 would be one length, a 50 would be two lengths, a 100 would be four lengths, etc
- **4 x 25:** Refers to the number of times a distance is to be done. For instance, in this example, 25 yards will be done four times
- **alternating 25s (or 50s) of:** Calls switching between two activities after a specific distance
- **Base:** The foundation of a training routine, usually representing the initial phase of training
- **Build:** Within a prescribed distance, increasing stroke tempo and speed steadily from start to finish
- **Breath Control:** Swimming or pulling with fewer than normal breaths as directed
- **Breathing Sequence:** The assigned breathing pattern, by number of strokes

- **Challenge:** A high expectation that requires physical and mental focus and determination to meet
- **Choice:** Swimmer chooses the stroke or kick
- **Cool Down:** The final exercise period of easy, continuous swimming that is important to gradually return the heart to its regular rhythm and rinse out the muscles
- **Descending:** Within a set of multiple swims, performing the second faster than the first and the third faster than the second, etc, so the times descend, while the effort ascends
- **Dolphin:** The motion used with Butterfly that starts high in the body and flows down through the feet
- **Drill:** An exercise designed to practice a specific skill or aspect of a stroke correctly
- **Drill/Swim:** An exercise that alternates given distances of drill and given distances of swim in order to use the skills emphasized in the drill in practice while swimming the full stroke
- **Fast Freestyle (or other stroke):** Using a faster tempo and applying more power to move across the pool faster than usual
- **Fins:** Devices worn on the feet for Dolphin or Flutter kick. When used properly fins can give the swimmer the experience of speed and lift, provide excellent aerobic work and promote ankle flexibility. When used improperly, fins can make kicking too easy.
- **Flutter Kick:** The kick done with Freestyle and Backstroke, using an alternating leg action
- **Hands leading:** The floating position with the hands extended beyond the head, leading the way
- **Head leading:** The floating position with the hands at the sides, so the head leads the way
- **IM:** Abbreviation of Individual Medley, the swimming event that includes Butterfly, Backstroke, Breaststroke and Freestyle, or any other stroke, in that order
- **Interval:** A predetermined time for a set of repetitions that represents the swim time plus the rest time
- **Kick:** Leg action only. A kickboard may be used for front flutter kick, or breaststroke kick. However, backstroke kick and dolphin kick should always be done without a kickboard.

- **Non-free:** Referring to Butterfly, Backstroke or Breaststroke
- **Pace:** A particular rate of speed continued over time
- **Pull:** Using a pull buoy to float your lower body, practice the upper body action of the stroke, including arm stroke, roll, alignment and use of core. For freestyle pulling only.
- **streamline position:** Floating with arms extended and squeezing ears, chin tucked, core firm and spine straight in order to minimize drag
- **Stroke Specialty:** The stroke that the swimmer specializes in
- **Swim:** Coordinated action of arm stoke, kicking and breathing as specified
- **w/15 (or other number) SR:** Refers to the amount of rest (R) in seconds (S) between swims. For example, in this case: with 15 seconds rest
- **Warm up:** Initial exercise period of sustained, medium intensity swimming lasting at least ten minutes, or at least 10% of your total yardage. Also an opportunity to review what you covered in your previous workout and to refresh your "feel" for the water
- **w/Fins:** Wearing fins to do flutter or dolphin kick
- **your favorite:** Swimmer chooses the drill

Workout Presentation

Each workout begins with a Challenge, and ends with the Total Yardage. Swimmers should focus on the challenge throughout the workout. Challenges are designed to prepare the swimmer for competition through practice in goal affirmation, positive self-talk, focus, adapting to unexpected situations and visualizing optimal performance. Total yardage is included as one measure of a training routine. All of the workouts in this book total between 4,000 and 6,000 yards/meters. It is important to remember that the main measure of this collection of workouts is not miles swum, but how the swimmer responds to the challenge.

Workout content is presented in a sequential format – one activity after the other – using a standardized set of directions. Each activity or set appears as a string of commands. Following is a explanation of the format.

1. First, the type of activity is stated, followed by a colon, like this:

2. Next, the distance and, if more than one, the quantity of repeats is stated.

3. Then, the actual activity is stated, like this:

Swim:
Kick:

4 x 50 Freestyle descending on :50
300 your choice

Drill/Swim: 200 alternating 25s of "Catch Up"/Freestyle

6. When a double space between activities or sets appears, it means take a rest, reflect on the activities you have done, and prepare for the next one.

5. Refers to the interval (swim + rest) that the swimmer will swim the set on.

4. Sometimes, a variation of the particular activity is called for.

Figure 2
Explanation of workout format

Drills with a Purpose

Stroke drills are a regular component of this collection of workouts. Drills are important at all levels of swimming! They provide an excellent way to improve stroke efficiency and "water handling," as well as working on a particular aspect of a stroke by isolating, emphasizing or repeating a drill exercise. To make the most of drill practice, it is important to understand the purpose of each drill.

Throughout these workouts, swimmers are asked to select their favorite drills, frequently from a particular category that represents the emphasis or purpose of the drill. Those categories are:
- **Balance** – the body's floating position
- **Alignment** – the body's line forward from finger tips to toes
- **Leverage** – using the largest muscle groups to access the most potential power

- **Stroke Path** – how the arm moves from front to back
- **Feel** – how the swimmer holds on to the water
- **Coordination** – how the multiple stroke actions work together

Below are a selection of effective drills, categorized by stroke and main purpose. Each drill is accompanied by a brief description of how to perform it. Most of these drills are also described in complete detail in the book, "The 100 Best Swimming Drills," by Blythe Lucero. This is an excellent resource to accompany this collection of workouts. In addition to step-by-step descriptions, each drill is illustrated, and its purpose is clearly outlined. Feedback charts also follow each drill, to address common problems that can interfere with feeling the point of the drills.

FREESTYLE DRILLS

BALANCE

Log Roll – Floating in a head lead position, and kicking continuously, go a quarter roll, hold for 5 seconds, do a quarter roll, continue, generate actions from the hips and stabilize from the core to practice balance and core centered swimming

Shark Fin – To practice a well balanced recovery, float on your side, low arm leading, and kick continuously. Raise the elbow of the high-side recovering arm to a high pointing position, then return arm it to your side. Repeat to the end of the pool, then switch arms

12 Kick Switch – To feel balance and length of the stroke, kick on side for twelve kicks, low arm leading, other arm at your side, face in the water, then switch sides, and arm positions, and repeat

ALIGNMENT

6 Kick Switch – To feel length of stroke and alignment, kick on side for six kicks, low arm leading, other arm at your side, face in the water, then switch sides, and arm positions, and repeat

3 Kick Switch – To practice maintaining good alignment while producing the rolling action of the stroke. Kick on side for three kicks, low arm leading, other arm at your side, face in the water, then switch sides, and arm positions and repeat

3 Strokes, 6 Kicks – To emphasize the non-flat, rolling body position and forward alignment, take three regular freestyle strokes with kicking, then kick only in the side floating position, low arm leading, other arm at your side, for six extra kicks, face in the water, then do three more freestyle strokes, then kick only floating on the other side for six extra kicks, and repeat

STROKE PATH

Dead Arm Freestyle – Single arm freestyle with the still arm at your side, breathing toward the still arm side, to practice the path of the stroke, using hip rotation to breathe

Push/Pull Freestyle – Regular freestyle isolating the pulling motion from full extension to the shoulder, and the pushing motion from the shoulder to the end of the stroke past the hip

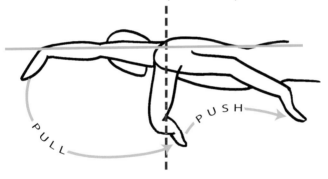

Figure 3
Pull/Push Freestyle.
Pull when your hand is in front of your shoulder.
Push when it is behind of your shoulder.

One Arm Freestyle – Single arm freestyle with the still arm leading to isolate the arm stroke action

LEVERAGE

3 Strokes, 3 Kicks – To emphasize the rolling action of the stroke, and available leverage obtained through switching sides. Take three regular freestyle strokes with kicking, then kick only in the side floating position, low arm leading, other arm at your side, for three extra kicks, face in the water, then do three more freestyle strokes, then kick only floating on the other side, and repeat

Hip Skating – Regular freestyle with an imaginary ice skate on each hip bone in front. Achieve a skating rhythm to practice core leverage

Pendulum – To feel leverage, switch rhythmically from one side floating position, with low are leading, and other arm in high elbow recovery position, to the other side, continue

Figure 4
Pendulum Drill
By rolling from side to side rhythmically, the swimmer
can feel the pendulum effect.

FEEL

All Thumbs Drill – Freestyle arm stroke extension actively pitching the wrist so the thumbs to point in the direction you are swimming for better catch

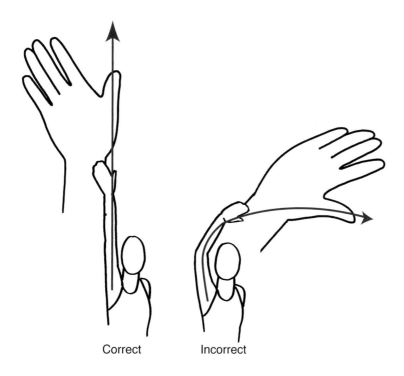

Correct   Incorrect

Figure 5
All Thumbs Drill
Point straight ahead, in the direction you are going
with the thumb of your reaching hand.
Allow your fingers to reach outward to catch more water.

Fist Freestyle – Freestyle with fists, using the forearms to press against the water to develop a high elbow underwater arm stroke

Sculling – Tracing a sideways figure eight with the hands, press out with thumbs down, press in with thumbs up, in order to develop better "feel" for the water

COORDINATION

Catch Up – Like regular freestyle, except one arm catches up to the other in front, emphasizing that one arm should always be reaching and the other stroking. Start with both arms leading, then do a complete freestyle stroke with one arm, when both arms are back in the leading position, do a freestyle stroke with the other arm, continue

Freestyle with Dolphin – Regular freestyle arms with a dolphin kick each time your hand strikes the water in front, to practice coordinating the arm and leg actions

Heads Up Freestyle – Rapid freestyle with your head up, as used in water polo, looking straight ahead to practice coordinating arm and leg action

BACKSTROKE DRILLS

BALANCE

Float on Spine w/Kick – Head lead kicking on back, floating on straight spine by rolling pelvis forward and contracting abdominals, so it feels like you are shaped like a banana, for better stroke balance

Cup on Forehead – Quarter Turn – To achieve a still or "independent head," do head leading backstroke kicking, with a cup half filled with water balancing on your forehead. Every twelve kicks, rotate your body a quarter turn, without dropping the cup. First to left, then back to flat, then to right, then back to flat, continue

Opposition Freeze Frame – Regular backstroke, stopping at various times in the stroke to feel the many balance points of the opposing arm stroke

ALIGNMENT

Clock Arms – First done standing in front of a mirror, practice feeling the correct hand entry position at shoulder width or wider (at least 11:00 and 1:00). Repeat while swimming backstroke

Backstroke 6 Kick Switch – To feel alignment, and the length of the stroke, kick on side for six kicks, low arm leading, other arm at your side, face up, then switch sides, and arm positions

Locked Elbow Recovery Drill – Backstroke, recovering with actively locked elbows for better alignment and stroke balance

STROKE PATH

One Arm Pull/Push Backstroke – Single arm backstroke, with still arm at your side, trying to isolate the pulling motion from full extension to the shoulder and the pushing motion from the shoulder to the end of the stroke past the hip

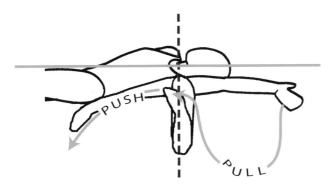

> **Figure 6**
> **One Arm Backstroke Pull/Push**
> **Pull when your hand is above your shoulder.**
> **Push when your hand is below your shoulder.**

One Arm Rope Climb – Floating on your back, with a lane line or rope beside you, take hold of the line and pull your body past the point where you are holding, simulating the feeling of efficient backstroke

Up and Over – Practicing the path of the backstroke arm stroke, where you catch deep then move your hand up and over your stationary elbow, then press the hand past the hip

LEVERAGE

Armpit Lift – Exaggerating the roll of the backstroke to feel that the high recovering side provides leverage to the low stroking side of the body.

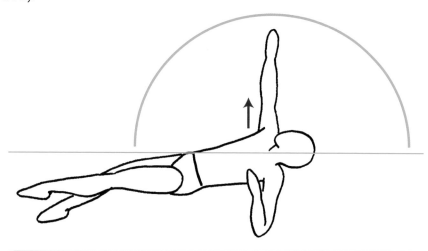

Figure 7
Armpit Lift
At the high point of each recovery, raise the armpit of your recovering arm completely out of the water.
Feel the leverage produced benefit your underwater arm.

Backstroke 3 Stroke Switch – To feel the rolling action of the stroke, kick on side for three kicks, low arm leading, other arm at your side, face up, then switch sides, and arm positions

Backstroke Balance Drill with Cup – Regular backstroke with a cup filled half way with water balancing on your forehead to emphasize that the head should be still, while the body rolls smoothly through the stroke

FEEL

Fist Backstroke – Backstroke with fists, using the forearms to press against the water to develop a high elbow arm stroke

Corkscrew – One stroke freestyle, then one stroke backstroke, continue, to feel the deep catch of the backstroke accomplished by rolling into your stroke

Dog Ears – Regular backstroke, pitching the hands actively outward from the wrist during recovery to maintain a relaxed hand, rather than an inwardly pitched "collapsed wrist." Achieving a positive wrist position will set up an aligned entry and good catch

COORDINATION

Breathing Pocket – Regular backstroke exaggerating the roll to feel a barrier from the water when the shoulder is at its highest point and using this moment to inhale

Roll,Pull/Roll,Push – Regular backstroke feeling that the continuous rolling action provides momentum and leverage to the pull and the push of the arm stroke. Roll down to catch and pull, roll up to transition and push

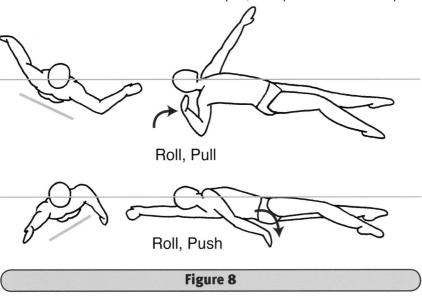

Roll, Pull

Roll, Push

Figure 8

Rhythmic Breathing – Practicing patterns of breathing in backstroke, including 1) inhale on one stroke, exhale on the other, 2) inhale and exhale during each recovery and, 3) inhale during one stroke cycle, and exhale on the next, to make rhythmic breathing as a regular part of your backstroke

BREASTSTROKE DRILLS

BALANCE

Fold and Shrug – Regular breaststroke where you focus on increasing your momentum into recovery by shrugging your shoulders up as you breathe and finish the in sweep, then rolling them down and forward into your quick, streamlined recovery

Eyes on the Water – Regular breaststroke where you look down at the water while inhaling, rather than forward, in order to continue the forward line of the stroke

Inhale at the High Point – Regular breaststroke where you achieve the breathing position through a combination of the lift from the accelerating arm stroke and the rocking motion of the stroke, rather than raising the head independently, or pressing down on the water

ALIGNMENT

Thread the Needle – Regular breaststroke where after each stroke you try to make a small hole in the water with your hands, then pass through that same hole with your elbows, shoulders and head, chest, hips, legs and feet, to feel the most streamlined stroke

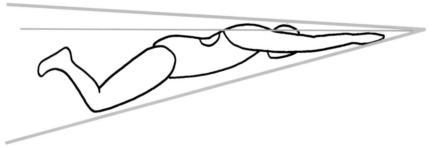

Figure 9
Thread the Needle
For the most streamlined stroke, your whole body should
follow your hands, as if through the eye of a needle.

Glide Length, Glide Speed – Regular breaststroke focusing on starting the next stroke at the exact point needed to maintain momentum. Too soon, and you do not benefit from the length or speed of the glide, too long, and you lose momentum

Tennis Ball Drill – Regular breaststroke holding a tennis ball under your chin, to practice maintaining a stable head position for the most productive forward motion

STROKE PATH

Corners Drill – Regular breaststroke, focusing on achieving lift for the breathing without pressing down on the water, but instead, by accelerating from the out sweep into the in sweep and holding on to the water well during the transition from one to the other.

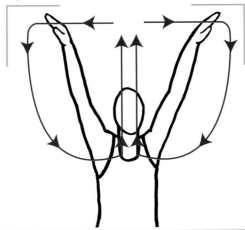

Figure 10
Corners Drill
Rather than pulling, sweep the hands out to their widest point, then, holding on to the water, "turn the corner" and sweep inward quickly under the chest and chin, then recover forward.

Half Breaststroke – Regular breaststroke progressively reducing the width and depth of the arm stroke so your hands and forearms stay within your rage of sight at all times, avoiding a dropped elbow "chicken wing" position, in order to get the most forward motion, with the least drag

Heads Up Breaststroke Arms with Flutter Kick – To be able to isolate the path of the arm stroke, and watch it, while feeling lift in the stroke, and still have the benefit of kick momentum

LEVERAGE

Breaststroke with Dolphin – Breaststroke arm stroke with a dolphin as you press out, and another as you sweep in, emphasizing the rocking action and core use in the breaststroke

Breaststroke Alternating Dolphin and Breaststroke Kick – Breaststroke arm stroke with a dolphin as you press out, and another dolphin as you sweep in, then, a complete breaststroke arm stroke, breath, breaststroke kick and glide, and repeat, alternating each armstroke with dolphin and breaststroke kick, to emphasize the rocking action and core use in the breaststroke

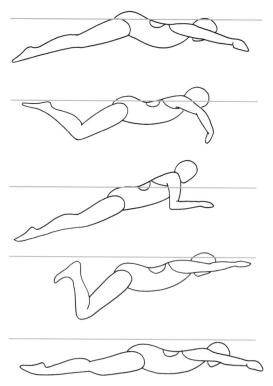

Figure 11
Breaststroke Alternating Dolphin and Breaststroke Kick

Stroke Up to Breathe, Kick Down to Glide – Regular breaststroke focusing on stroking and breathing while rocking up, and then kicking while rocking down, to emphasize stroke leverage

FEEL

Breaststroke with Fists – Breaststroke arm stroke with fists, using the forearms to press against the water to develop a stable, high elbow position on out sweep and to use the full paddle available on the in sweep

Breaststroke Sculling – Press out with thumbs down, press in with thumbs up, in order to develop better "feel" for lateral motion of the breaststroke arm stroke

Hand Speed Drill – To practice no pauses in the arm stroke, especially at the "drag point" that can occur at the transition from in sweep and recovery. Do breaststroke arm stroke with flutter kick, trying to accomplish a complete arm stroke (out sweep, in sweep, recovery) within the time it takes to do four flutter kick downbeats, then hold in streamline for six kicks and continue

COORDINATION

3 Kick Breaststroke – To emphasize that each stroke begins and ends in a streamline position, float in a hand lead position and do three breaststroke kicks in a row, then do one complete stroke cycle of arm stroke, breathing, kick, glide and repeat

No Stars – Regular breaststroke avoiding stroking and kicking at the same time. Stroke and then kick, repeat to achieve stroke timing that will produce the least drag

Shoot to Streamline – Regular breaststroke where you focus on accelerating through the drag point of the stroke, just after the insweep, and use that momentum to get back to the streamline position

BUTTERFLY DRILLS

BALANCE

Weight Shifting – In a head leading floating position, do a bowing motion, hips constantly high, feeling how your weight shifts forward as you bow down and back as you bow up, creating a shifting body balance that produces forward motion

Chest Balance – Regular butterfly focusing on the point when your chest is at its lowest point. You should feel as if you are riding downhill and forward for an instant before you start your arm stroke and your chest rises. This balance point adds leverage to the stroke that would not be present from a flat body position

Pinkies Up – Regular butterfly focusing on maintaining a consistent "pinkie up" hand position during recovery, so the elbows do not drag through the water, but rather the arms make an arch over the water's surface

ALIGNMENT

Reaching to a "Y" – Regular butterfly focusing on a wide "Y" shaped entry, leading with the thumbs in order to produce the most aligned position to start the stroke, and the best catch

Hammer and Nail – Regular butterfly, breathing each stroke, imagining that your forehead is a hammer and the water is a nail. When your head returns to the water, strike the nail with force. Avoid striking the water with your chin, which will lead to frontal drag

Eyes on the Water Butterfly – Regular butterfly where you look down at the water while inhaling, rather than forward, in order to continue the forward line of the stroke

STROKE PATH

Sweeping Question Marks – Regular butterfly tracing the path of the butterfly arms, wide to narrow, and shallow to deep, in order to practice the front to back sweep of the arm stroke

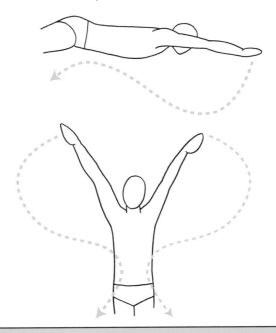

Figure 12
Sweeping Question Marks
The path of the butterfly arm stroke underwater makes the shape of a question mark and its reflection both wide to narrow and deep to shallow.

One Arm Butterfly – From a hand leading position, do butterfly with one arm only, while the other arm remains extended, to practice butterfly stroke rhythm, the pull and push of the arm stroke, and focus on keeping the hips up in a more sustainable manner than the full stroke

Left Arm, Right Arm, Both Arms – From a hand leading position, do one butterfly stroke with your left arm only, then one with your right arm, then a stroke with both arms. Start each new stroke when the previous stroke returns to the starting point. To practice butterfly stroke path, rhythm, and to bridge from drill to swim

LEVERAGE

Advanced One Arm Butterfly – From a head leading position, do butterfly with one arm only, while the other arm remains at your side, to practice butterfly leverage, stroke rhythm, the pull and push of the arm stroke, and focus on getting the chest down in a more sustainable manner than the full stroke

No Pause Butterfly – Also known as "Grab and Go Butterfly", where you swim four to eight strokes of butterfly, with absolutely no hesitation between the extension and the catch, the point momentum is commonly lost. Then finish the length in easy freestyle and repeat

No Kick Butterfly – Regular butterfly except consciously do not kick. Keep your hips up and raise and dip your chest and notice that the kick flows down to your feet anyway. This drill emphasizes initiating the kick from high in the body, rather than from the feet

FEEL

Pitch to Press – Regular butterfly practicing pressing back on the water, rather than down and to maintain constant pressure on the water by changing the pitch of your hands throughout the path of the stroke. Start with your hands extended in the butterfly entry position. Do an butterfly arm stroke, pressing out and back, then sweeping in and back, then again pressing out and back, repeat

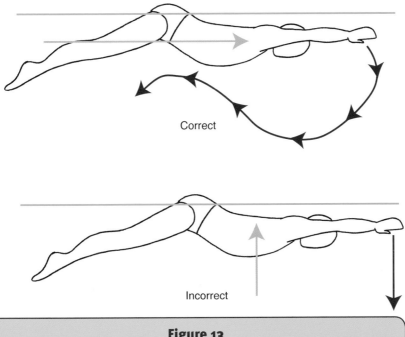

Correct

Incorrect

Figure 13
Pitch to Press
Pitch your hands to press back on the water,
rather than down, to move your body forward.

Freestyle with Dolphin – Regular freestyle arms with a dolphin kick each time your hand strikes the water in front. Notice that the other arm will be finishing the push phase of the arm stroke at the same time. An excellent and sustainable drill for stroke path as well as kick timing.

Round Off – Regular butterfly focusing on finishing the arm stroke by pressing outward, like a "J" from the hips, for easy release from the water and a quick transition to recovery

COORDINATION

Quiet Butterfly – Regular butterfly focusing on using the water, not fighting it. At entry, lay your hands quietly out on the surface of the water, fingertips extended and anchor your hands just below the surface of the water as your feet snap down with power, but without splash. Sweep through and bring the momentum of the pull and push of the stroke, and second dolphin into a fluid but silent recovery.

The Flop – Regular butterfly focusing on initiating the recovery from the shoulders to achieve a relaxed forward reaching recovery. Release the water, pinkies up, swing arms wide and around from the shoulders, not the hands, until your arms are at shoulder level. Then, roll your shoulders forward and redirect your hands to reach forward, and as they do drop your chest into the water.

Coordination Checkpoint – Regular butterfly focusing on coordinating three actions so they occur at exactly the same time: the round off finish of the underwater arm stroke, the downward snap of the second kick, and the inhale.

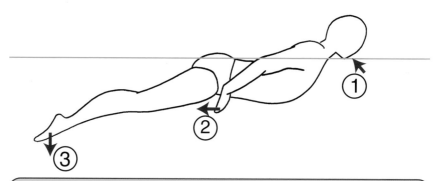

Figure 14
Coordination Checkpoint.
Three things happen at once:
end of the inhale, the end of the push
and the end of the second dolphin

CHALLENGE WORKOUTS

The following workouts are appropriate for early season base work or as freestyle specialty training material. Contents include general endurance and aerobic work, interval training, speed play and breath control work. Swim distances range from 25 to 500 yards/meters. Set distances range from 500 to 2,000 yards/meters. Workouts distances range from 4,100 to 6,000 yards/meters. Warm up and Cool down distances are shown as the minimum distance recommended.

Approach each workout with three goals:

1. Make the most of each workout challenge presented throughout the session by mentally engaging in goal affirmation, positive self-talk, focusing on the task at hand, controlling, adapting and visualizing.

2. Perform each workout with effort that challenges your fitness level and quality that reinforces for swimming efficiency.

3. Have fun with it!

1Workout

Challenge: State your goal as begin the workout and again when you finish the workout in less than 80 minutes.

Warm up:	500
Kick:	8 x 50 Flutter or Dolphin on 1:00
Swim:	8 x 75 alternating 25s of Free/Non-free/Free on 1:15
Swim:	5 x 100 Free on 1:30
Swim:	5 x 100 Free on 1:25
Swim:	5 x 100 Free on 1:20
100 Easy	
Kick:	200 Choice
Pull:	400
Swim:	8 x 25 Choice on :30
Cool down:	200
Total:	4,100

2 Workout

Challenge: Start strong, finish strong, saying to yourself, "I am doing what it takes."

Warm up:	500
Kick/Swim:	500 – alternating 50s of Flutter/Free
Swim:	10 x 50 Free on :50 – Build

Swim
100 Easy
3 x 500 on 7:00

	8 x 100 Free on 1:30
	Swim – alternating 25s of Free/Choice
	Pull – breathing sequence: by 25 – every 3, 5, 7, 9...
	Swim – all Free
Kick:	4 x 25 w/fins on :30

Cool down:	200
Total:	4,200

3Workout

Challenge: Concentrate on each set, then move on to the next.

Warm up:	500
Kick:	4 x 100 Flutter on 15/SR
Swim:	3 x 200 Free on 3:00
Swim:	6 x 100 Free on 1:30
Swim:	12 x 50 Free on :45
100 Easy	
Kick:	200
Kick:	200 w/Fins – streamline position
Pull:	500
Kick/Swim:	6 x 50 – alternating 25s of Kick/Swim – choice on 1:00
Cool down:	200
Total:	4,200

4 Workout

Challenge: How would you respond positively if you get caught in traffic on the way to your big swim meet?

Warm up:	500
Kick:	4 x 100 Flutter on 15/SR
Drill:	200 – your favorite Coordination Drill
Swim:	200 Free – for time
Swim:	8 x 200 on 3:15 – each 200 includes one length of kick only – Match your 200 time above.
100 Easy	
Swim:	16 x 50 – alternating 50s of Free/Non-free on :45/1:00
Kick:	8 x 25 w/Fins on :30 – streamline position
Cool down:	200
Total:	4,200

5 Workout

Challenge: Maintain a narrow descend, visualizing energy and power.

Warm up:	500
Kick:	200 Flutter
Kick:	200 Dolphin
Kick:	200 w/Fins – streamline position
Swim:	5 x 200 Free – Descending on 3:00
Swim:	10 x 50 on 1:00 – alternating 25s of Free/Non-free
Swim:	5 x 100 Free – Descending on 1:30
100 Easy	
Swim:	4 x 100 Free – Descending on 1:30
	(starting time: #3 of previous set)
100 Easy	
Swim:	3 x 100 Free – Descending on 1:30
	(starting time: #3 of previous set)
100 Easy	
Swim:	8 x 25 Choice – alternating 25 of Fast/Easy
	on :30/1:00, Descending fast 25s
Cool down:	200
Total:	4,500

6Workout

Challenge: Swim your goal pace.

Warm up:	500
Kick:	200 Flutter
Drill:	200 – your favorite Leverage Drill
Kick:	200 w/Fins – streamline position
Swim	8 x 25 – Build on :30
Swim	8 x 50 – Build on :45
Swim:	10 x 150 Free on 2:15
100 Easy	
Swim:	20 x 50 – alternating 50s of Free/Non-free on :50
Cool down:	200
Total:	4,500

7Workout

Challenge: Repeat to yourself, "I have the power."

Warm up:	500
Kick:	500 – alternating 25s of Flutter/Dolphin
Swim:	20 x 50 Free on :45
100 Easy	
Pull:	500 – Breathing Sequence: by 25 – every 3, 5, 7, 9...
Swim:	10 x 100 Free – with one length Non-free on 1:30
100 Easy	
Kick:	200 Choice
Kick:	8 x 50 – w/Fins on :45 – streamline position
Cool down:	200
Total:	4,500

8 Workout

Challenge: If your quality slips, RE-FOCUS!

Warm up:	500
Kick:	200
Swim:	8 x 50 Choice – Build on 1:00
Kick:	300 w/Fins – streamline position
Swim:	10 x 200 Free on 3:00
100 Easy	
Kick:	200 Choice
Swim:	8 x 50 Choice – Build on 1:00
Kick:	300 w/Fins – streamline position
Cool down:	200
Total:	4,600

Workout

Challenge: How would you respond positively if you found out the pool was closing in 1 hour?

Warm up:	500
Kick/Swim:	20 x 50 – alternating 50s Kick/Swim w/10 SR
Swim	4 x 400 w/40 SR:
	1. every 4th length fast
	2. 400 – every 3rd length fast
	3. 400 – every other length fast
	4. 400: All fast
100 Easy	
Swim:	8 x 75 – middle length Non-free on 2:15
Swim:	8 x 75 – first and last lengths Non-free on 2:30
Cool down:	200
Total:	4,600

10 Workout

Challenge: Visualize feeling light and fast.

Warm up:	500
Drill:	200 your favorite Alignment Drill
Kick:	8 x 50 Flutter on 1:00
Kick:	200 your favorite Feel Drill
Swim:	4 x 50 Free on Interval -5 sec
100 Easy	
Swim:	4 x 100 Free on Interval -5 sec
100 Easy	
Swim:	6 x 50 Free on Interval -5 sec
100 Easy	
Swim:	6 x 100 Free on Interval -5 sec
100 Easy	
Swim:	8 x 50 Free on Interval -5 sec
100 Easy	
Swim:	8 x 100 Free on Interval -5 sec
Cool down:	200
Total:	4,700

11 Workout

Challenge: Show your commitment to your goal under and over the water.

Warm up:	500
Kick:	200
Drill:	300 – your favorite Alignment Drill
Kick:	10 x 50 w/Fins on :45 – streamline position
Swim:	6 x 100 Free on 1:30 – 4 dolphins off each wall
Pull:	300 – Breathing Sequence: by 25 – every 3, 5, 7, 9 ...
Swim:	6 x 100 Free on 1:30 – 6 dolphins off each wall
Pull:	300 – Breathing Sequence: by 25 – every 3, 5, 7, 9 ...
Swim:	6 x 100 Free on 1:30 – 8 dolphins off each wall
100 Easy	
Kick:	200
Swim:	10 x 50 Free/Non-Free on 1:00 – extend streamline off each wall
Cool down:	200
Total:	4,800

12 **Workout**

Challenge: Think of 3 power words to motivate you when the workout gets tough.

Warm up:	500
Kick:	200 Flutter
Drill/Swim:	500 – alternating 25s of your favorite Feel Drill/Swim
Kick:	10 x 50 w/Fins on :45 – streamline position
Swim:	4 x 200 on 3:00 – match your time on 200 #1 & 2, and #3 & 4
100 Easy	
Swim	20 x 100 on 1:30 – match times on #1 & 2, #3 & 4, #5 & 6...
Cool down:	200
Total:	4,800

13 Workout

Challenge: Use active recovery to focus on the fast swims to come.

Warm up:	500
Kick:	300 Flutter
Kick:	300 Dolphin
Swim:	4 x 400 w/40 SR – timed
	1. 50 Fast, 50 Easy ...
	2. 75 Fast, 25 Easy ...
	3. 25 Fast, 25 Easy ...
	4. All Fast – compare to other times
100 Easy	
Kick:	10 x 50 w/Fins on 1:00 – streamline position
Swim:	10 x 50 Non-Free on 1:00
Swim:	10 x 50 Free on :45
Kick:	10 x 50 w/Fins on 1:00 – streamline position
Cool down:	200
Total:	5,000

14 Workout

Challenge: How would you respond positively if the clock stopped in the middle of a set?

Warm	up: 500
Kick:	200 Flutter
Drill:	200 – your favorite Alignment Drill
Kick:	500 w/Fins – streamline position
Swim:	24 x 100 on 1:30 – Free, Choice, Pull...
100 Easy	
Kick:	500 w/Fins – streamline position
Swim:	16 x 25 on :30 – alternating Free/Choice
Cool down:	200
Total:	5,000

15 Workout

Challenge: Visualize moving through the water at a rate of one body length per second.

Warm up:	500
Kick:	300 Flutter or Dolphin
Drill:	500 – alternating 25s of your favorite Leverage Drill/Swim
Swim:	12 x 75 Free w/15 SR – Build
Pull:	500 – Breathing Sequence: by 25 – every 3, 5, 7, 9…
Swim:	10 x 100 Free on 1:30 – count strokes
Swim:	8 x 100 Free on 1:30 – w/1-2 fewer strokes per length, maintaining time

100 Easy
Swim: 8 x 50 Free on :45 – maintain best stroke count

Cool down:	200
Total:	5,200

Workout

Challenge: How will you show your commitment to your goal in this workout?

Warm up:	500
Kick/Drill:	300 – alternating 25s of Flutter Kick/your favorite Coordination Drill
Kick:	300 w/Fins – streamline position
Swim:	16 x 50 Free on :50 – Build 1-8, Descend 9-12, 13-16
Swim:	6 x 200 on 3:00 – alternating 200s of Free/Non-free
100 Easy	
Swim:	8 x 100 Free on 1:30
Swim:	6 x 100 Free on 1:25
Swim:	4 x 100 Free on 1:20
100 Easy	
Cool down:	200
Total:	5,300

17 Workout

Challenge: Say to yourself, "I swim with rhythm and grace."

Warm up:	500
Kick:	300 Flutter or Dolphin
Drill:	400 – alternating 25s of your favorite Leverage Drill/Swim
Swim:	12 x 50 Free on :50 – Build
Swim:	9 x 200 on 3:00 – alternate 200s of Free, Pull, Non-free
100 Easy	
Swim:	20 x 50 on :50 – alternating 50s of Fast strokes/ Long strokes
100 Easy	
Kick:	16 x 25 w/Fins on :30 – streamline position
Cool down:	200
Total:	5,400

18 Workout

Challenge: Channel your energy into each new swim.

Warm up:	500
Kick:	300 Flutter
Drill/Swim:	500 – alternating 25s of your favorite Feel Drill/ Swim
Swim:	12 x 100 Free on 1:30 – Descend 1 – 4, 5 – 8, 9 – 12
Swim:	6 x 100 Non-free on 1:40
100 Easy	
Kick:	500 w/Fins – streamline position
Pull:	500 – Breathing Sequence: by 25 – every 3, 5, 7, 9 ...
Swim:	20 x 50 on :50 – first 25 Non-free, second 25 Free
Cool down:	200
Total:	5,400

Workout

Challenge: How would you respond positively if your goggles broke in the middle of your event?

Warm up:	500
Kick:	300 Flutter or Dolphin
Drill:	400 – your favorite Coordination Drill
Kick:	500 w/Fins – streamline position
Swim:	5 x 100 Free on 1;30
Swim:	500 Free
Swim:	5 x 100 Free on 1:30
Swim:	500 Free
100 Easy	
Kick:	200 Choice
Swim:	8 x 50 Non-free on :50
Swim:	8 x 50 Free on :45
Swim:	8 x 50 – 25 Non-free, 25 Free on :45
Cool down:	200
Total:	5,600

Workout

Challenge: Visualize feeling calm and loose before your event.

Warm up:	500
Drill/Swim:	400 – alternating 25s of your favorite Coordination Drill/Swim
Swim:	8 x 50 Free – Descending on :50
Swim:	6 x 50 Free – Descending on :45
Swim:	4 x 50 Free – Descending on :40
100 Easy	
Kick:	200 Choice
Swim:	6 x 100 Free – Descending on 1:30
Swim:	5 x 100 Free – Descending on 1:25
Swim:	4 x 100 Free – Descending on 1:20
100 Easy	
Kick:	200 Choice
Swim:	4 x 200 Free – Descending on 3:00
Swim:	3 x 200 Free – Descending on 2:55
Swim:	2 x 200 Free – Descending on 2:50
Cool down:	200
Total:	5,800

21 Workout

Challenge: Where are you on the path to your goal?

Warm up:	500
Kick:	200
Drill:	5 x 100 – alternating 25s of your favorite Feel Drill/Swim w/10 SR
Kick:	300 w/Fins – streamline position
Swim:	20 x 50 on :50 – every fourth 50 Non-free
Pull:	500 – Breathing Sequence: by 25 – every 3, 5, 7, 9 ...
100 Easy	
Swim:	5 x 100 on 1:30 – first length of each Non-free
Swim:	5 x 100 on 1:30 – last length of each is Non-free
100 Easy	
200 Kick	
Swim:	8 x 25 Choice on :30
Swim:	200 Free – timed
Swim:	8 x 25 Choice on :30
Swim:	200 Free – faster time
Swim:	8 x 25 Choice on :30
Swim:	200 Free – even faster time
Swim:	8 x 25 Choice on :30
Cool down:	200
Total:	6,000

Workout

Challenge: Say to yourself, "I deserve to achieve my goal."

Warm up:	500
Kick:	8 x 50 Flutter or Dolphin on 1:00
Drill:	– 400 your favorite Coordination Drill
Swim:	12 x 75 Free w/15 SR
	1-4: 50 Medium 25 Fast
	5-8: 25 Medium, 50 Fast
	9-12: All Fast

100 Easy

Swim:	6 x 200 Free with descending rest: :30, :25, :20, :15, :10 – maintain your time

100 Easy
200 Kick

Swim:	6 x 100 Free with descending rest: :30, :25, :20, :15, :10 – maintain your time

100 Easy
200 Kick

Swim:	6 x 50 Free with descending rest: :30, :25, :20, :15, :10 – maintain your time

100 Easy

Pull:	500 – Breathing Sequence: by 25 – every 3, 5, 7, 9…
Swim:	12 x 25 Choice on :30/:40 – Fast/Easy

Cool down: 200
Total: 6,000

23 Workout

Challenge: Clear your mind of distractions, and focus on your swimming.

Warm up:	500
Drill/Swim:	300 – alternating 25s of your favorite Leverage Drill/Swim
Kick:	8 x 50 your choice w/15 SR
Swim/Pull:	100, 200, 300, 400, 500, 400, 300, 200, 100 – alternating distances of Free/Pull w/30 SR
100 Easy Swim:	12 x 50 Free on :45
100 Easy Swim:	12 x 50 – alternating 25s of Free/Non-free on :50
100 Easy Swim:	12 x 50 Non-Free on :55
Cool down:	200
Total:	6,000

24 Workout

Challenge: How would you respond positively a crowded meet warm up situation?

Warm up:	500
Kick:	300 Flutter or Dolphin
Drill:	300 – your favorite Alignment Drill
Kick:	300 w/Fins
Swim	8 x 100 Free on 1:25
Swim:	4 x 200 Free on 2:55
Swim:	8 x 100 Free on 1:20
Swim:	4 x 200 Free on 2:50
100 Easy	
Pull:	500
Swim:	4 x 50 Free on :45
Swim:	4 x 50 Non-free on :50
Swim:	4 x 50 Free on :40
Cool down:	200
Total:	6,000

25 Workout

Challenge: Visualize an optimal race finish.

Warm up:	500
Kick:	10 x 50 Flutter or Dolphin on 1:00
Swim:	16 x 75 w/15 SR
	1-4: Build
	5-8: Pace
	9-12: Build
	13-16: Pace

100 Easy

Pull:	500 – Breathing Sequence: by 25 – every 3, 5, 7, 9 ...
Kick:	200 your choice
Swim:	5 x 200 w/20 SR
	1: Non-free
	2: Non-free w/last 50 Free
	3: Non-free w/last 100 Free
	4: Non-free w/last 150 Free
	5: Free

100 Easy

Kick:	500 w/Fins
Swim:	10 x 50 Free on :45
Swim:	8 x 50 Free on :40
Swim:	6 x 50 Free on :35
Cool down:	200
Total:	6,000

I.M. / STROKE SPECIALTY WORKOUTS

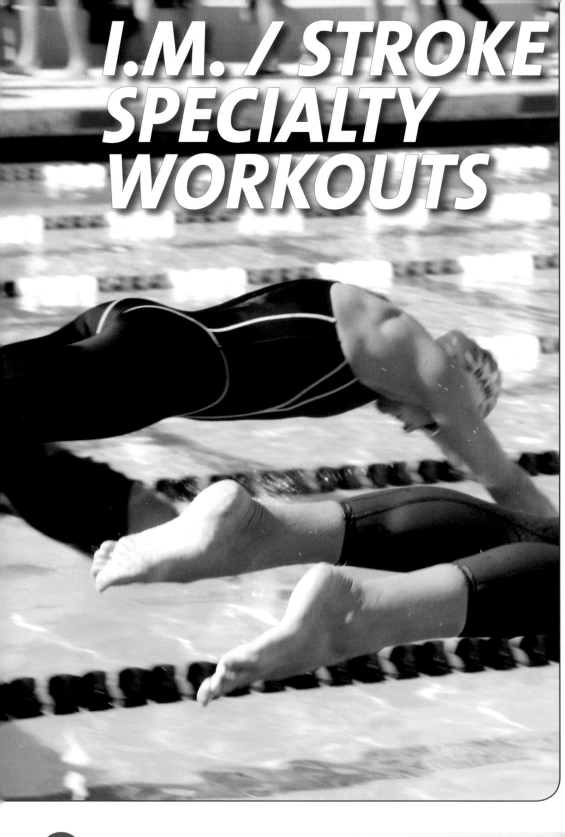

The following workouts are appropriate for Individual Medley or stroke specialty training. Contents include non-free and four stroke sets, strong stroke and weak stroke work, transition work, IM, and endurance swims. Swim distances range from 25 to 500 yards/meters. Set distances range from 500 to 2,000 yards/meters. Workouts distances range from 4,000 to 6,000 yards/meters. Warm up and Cool down distances are shown as the minimum distance recommended.

Approach each workout with three goals:

1. Make the most of each workout challenge presented throughout the session by mentally engaging in goal affirmation, positive self talk, focusing on the task at hand, controlling and adapting and visualizing.

2. Perform each workout with effort that challenges your fitness level and quality that reinforces for swimming efficiency.

3. Have fun with it!

Workout

Challenge: State, repeat and own the distance and stroke of your goal event.

Warm up:	500
Kick:	400 Flutter or Dolphin
Drill:	4 x 100 – your favorite, 100 of each stroke
Swim:	12 x 75 w/15 SR – middle length is IM order
100 Easy	
Swim:	4 x 200 w/20 SR – odd lengths IM order, even lengths Free
100 Easy	
Swim:	12 x 50 on 1:00 – alternating 50s of Stroke Specialty/Weakest Stroke
Cool down:	200
Total:	4,000

Workout 27

Challenge: Say to yourself, "I am stronger because I am more versatile."

Warm up:	500
Kick:	400 Flutter or Dolphin
Drill:	8 x 50 – your favorite, IM order w/15 SR

Swim:	3 x 100 on 1:30 – first length Fly
Swim:	3 x 100 on 1:30 – first length Back
Swim:	3 x 100 on 1:30 – first length Breast
100 Easy	
Swim:	3 x 100 on 1:30 – last length Fly
Swim:	3 x 100 on 1:30 – last length Back
Swim:	3 x 100 on 1:30 – last length Breast
100 Easy	
Swim:	10 x 50 Stroke Specialty on 1:00

Cool down:	200
Total:	4,000

Workout

Challenge: Find the unique rhythm in each set.

Warm up:	500
Kick:	300 – 100 IM sequence
Swim:	8 x 75 Stroke Specialty w/15 SR
Swim:	8 x 75 IM w/o Free w/15 SR
Swim:	8 x 75 Free w/15 SR
Swim:	8 x 75 Weakest Stroke w/15 SR
100 Easy	
Pull:	300
Kick:	8 x 25 w/Fins on :30 – streamline position
Cool down:	200
Total:	4,000

29 Workout

Challenge: Overcome the adversity of a "weak" stroke by improving it, and building strength around it.

Warm up:	500
Kick:	200 Flutter
Drill:	200 your favorite Freestyle Drill
Kick:	200 Flutter on Back
Drill:	200 your favorite Backstroke Drill
Kick:	200 Breaststroke Kick
Drill:	200 your favorite Breaststroke Drill
Kick:	200 Dolphin
Drill:	200 your favorite Butterfly Drill
Swim:	8 x 125 IM w/20 SR – double one stroke on each IM, rotating through
100 Easy	
Swim:	4 x 50 on 1:00 – 1st Stroke Specialty
Swim:	4 x 50 on 1:00 – 2nd Stroke Specialty
Swim:	4 x 50 on 1:00 – 3rd Stroke Specialty
Swim:	4 x 50 on 1:00 – 4th Stroke Specialty
Cool down:	200
Total:	4,100

Workout

Challenge: Visualize advancing through the water with power at the end of your IM.

Warm up:	500
Kick:	400 IM
Swim:	100 Free, 200 IM, 300 Free, 400 IM, 500 Free, 400 IM, 300 Free, 200 IM, 100 Free
100 Easy	
Kick:	200 your choice
Swim:	8 x 25 Stroke Specialty w/15 SR
Cool down:	200
Total:	4,100

34 Workout

Challenge: Affirm your commitment by building your weakest stroke.

Warm up:	500
Kick:	10 x 50 on 1:00 – alternating 50s of Flutter/Dolphin
Swim:	8 x 75 w/15 SR – first length of each is IM order
Swim:	8 x 75 w/15 SR – middle length of each is IM order
Swim:	8 x 75 w/15 SR – last length of each is IM order
100 Easy	
Swim:	200 Stroke Specialty
Swim:	100 Weakest Stroke
Swim:	200 Stroke Specialty
Swim:	100 Weakest Stroke
100 Easy	
Kick/Swim:	4 x 25 w/10 SR – Dolphin/Fly
Kick/Swim:	4 x 25 w/10 SR – Flutter on Back/Back
Kick/Swim:	4 x 25 w/10 SR – Breaststroke Kick/Breaststroke
Kick/Swim:	4 x 25 w/10 SR – Flutter/Freestyle
Cool down:	200
Total:	4,200

Workout

Challenge: Say to yourself, "I am leaving no stone unturned in my IM."

Warm up:	500
Kick:	10 x 50 on 1:00 – alternating 50s of Flutter/Dolphin
Drill/Swim:	200 – your favorite Stroke Specialty Drill/Stroke Specialty
Drill/Swim:	200 – your favorite weakest stroke Drill/Weakest stroke
Swim:	4 x 50 IM order on 1:00
Swim:	4 x 50 IM order on :55
Swim:	4 x 50 IM order on :50
Swim:	4 x 50 IM order on :45
100 Easy	
Swim:	4 x 250 w/20 SR – 25 Fly, 50 Back, 75 Breast, 100 Free
100 Easy	
Pull:	500
Swim:	8 x 25 Stroke Specialty on :30
Kick:	8 x 25 w/Fins – streamline position on :30
Cool down:	200
Total:	4,200

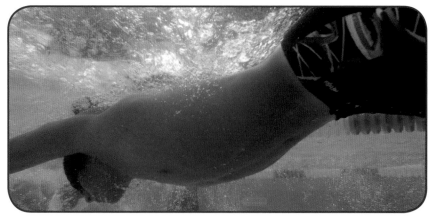

33 Workout

Challenge: Swim each IM as if it was the only one.

Warm up:	500
Kick:	400 IM
Drill/Swim:	8 x 50 on 1:00 – IM order, your favorite Drill/Swim
Swim:	5 x 400 IM w/60 SR
100 Easy	
Kick:	200 choice
Swim:	4 x 50 Stroke Specialty on :55
Swim:	4 x 50 Free on :45
Kick:	4 x 50 w/Fins – streamline position on: 45
Cool down:	200
Total:	4,400

34 Workout

Challenge: How would you respond positively to a ten minute delay at the blocks.

Warm up:	500
Kick:	200 Flutter
Kick:	200 Choice
Drill/Swim:	4 x 100 w/15 SR – IM order, your favorite Drill/Swim
Swim:	5 x 100 Stroke Specialty w/20 SR
Swim:	5 x 100 2nd Stroke w/20 SR
Swim:	5 x 100 3rd Stroke w/20 SR
Swim:	5 x 100 4th Stroke w/20 SR
100 Easy	
Kick:	10 x 50 Choice on 1:00 – fast
Cool down:	200
Total:	4,400

35 Workout

Challenge: Visualize seamless transitions.

Warm up:	500
Kick/Drill:	16 x 50 IM order – Kick/your favorite drill w/15 SR
Kick:	500 w/Fins – streamline position
Swim:	6 x 200 Free/Pull on 1:30
Swim:	8 x 100 w/20 SR
	1 & 5 50 Fly, 50 Back
	2 & 6 50 Back, 50 Breast
	3 & 7 50 Breast, 50 Free
	4 & 8 50 Free, 50 Fly
Kick:	200 Choice
Swim:	12 x 25 on :30 – alternating Stroke Specialty/ Weakest Stroke
Cool down:	200
Total:	4,500

Workout 36

Challenge: Affirm your commitment to being the most versatile swimmer possible.

Warm up:	500
Kick:	400 IM order
Drill:	400 IM order – your favorite Drills
Swim:	12 x 100 on 1:30 – every 4th 100 is your Stroke Specialty
100 Easy	
Swim:	200 IM
Swim:	4 x 25 Fly on :30
Swim:	200 IM
Swim:	4 x 25 Back on :30
Swim:	200 IM
Swim:	4 x 25 Breast on :30
Swim:	200 IM
Swim:	4 x 25 Free on :30
100 Easy	
Kick:	8 x 50 w/Fins – streamline position on 1:00
Cool down:	200
Total:	4,500

37 Workout

Challenge: Say to yourself, "I have four strong strokes."

Warm up:	500
Kick:	200 Flutter or Dolphin
Drill:	200 your favorite Leverage Drill
Swim:	6 x 100 Free on 1:30
Swim:	200 Fly
Swim:	6 x 100 Free on 1:30
Swim:	200 Back
Swim:	6 x 100 Free on 1:30
Swim:	200 Breast
Swim:	6 x 100 Free on 1:30
Swim:	200 Free
100 Easy	
Kick:	8 x 25 fast Flutter Kick w/10 SR
Cool down:	200
Total:	4,600

Workout 38

Challenge: Channel new energy into every new stroke.

Warm up:	500
Kick:	4 x 100 Flutter w/15 SR
Drill:	4 x 100 – your favorite, IM order w/15 SR
Swim:	12 x 75 w/15 SR – middle length IM order
100 Easy	
Swim:	4 x 200 IM w/30 SR – rotate through 50 kick
100 Easy	
Swim:	8 x 50 on :45 – Free
Swim:	8 x 50 on :50 – Stroke Specialty
Kick:	8 x 50 Stroke Specialty on 1:00
Cool down:	200
Total:	4,600

39 Workout

Challenge: No stroke should phase you.

Warm up:	500
Kick:	500 alternate 50s of Flutter/Stroke Specialty Kick
Drill/Swim:	400 IM order – alternating 25s of your favorite Drill/Swim
Swim/Pull:	6 x 200 – alternating 200s of Free/Pull on 3:00
100 Easy	
Swim:	100 IM – rest :15
Swim:	2 x 100 IM with no rest between them, then rest :20
Swim:	3 x 100 IM with no rest between them, then rest :25
Swim:	4 x 100 IM with no rest between them
100 Easy	
Kick:	200 Choice
Swim:	10 x 50 Stroke Specialty on :50
Cool down:	200
Total:	4,700

Workout

Challenge: Visualize your second wind.

Warm up:	500
Kick:	200 choice
Drill:	200 your favorite
Kick:	8 x 50 w/Fins – streamline position
Swim:	5 x 100 Free on 1:30 – Descending
Swim:	4 x 75 w/:15 SR – 50 Fly, 25 Back
Swim:	4 x 75 w/:15 SR – 50 Back, 25 Breast
Swim:	4 x 75 w/:15 SR – 50 Breast, 25 Free
Swim:	4 x 75 w/:15 SR – 50 Free, 25 Fly
100 Easy	
Pull:	500 – Breathing Sequence: by 25 – every 3, 5, 7, 9...
Swim:	5 x 100 Stroke Specialty w/15 SR
100 Easy	
Swim:	16 x 25 on :30 – 400 IM order
Cool down:	200
Total:	4,800

41 Workout

Challenge: State your goal 5 times during this workout.

Warm up:	500
Kick:	5 x 100 Flutter or Dolphin w/15 SR
Drill/Swim:	500 alternating 25s of your favorite Drill/Swim
Swim:	10 x 100 Free on 1:30
Swim:	5 x 100 Stroke Specialty on 1:40
	200 Kick – Choice
Swim:	10 x 100 Free on 1:25
Swim:	5 x 100 Stroke Specialty on 1:35
Cool down:	200
Total:	4,900

Workout

Challenge: Say to yourself, "I own the IM!"

Warm up:	500
Kick:	400 IM
Drill:	200 your favorite
Swim:	8 x 100 Free on 1:30
Swim:	8 x 50 Fly on :50
Swim:	6 x 100 Free on 1:25
Swim:	8 x 50 Back on :50
Swim:	4 x 100 Free on 1:20
Swim:	8 x 50 Breast on :50
Swim:	2 x 100 Free on 1:15
Swim:	8 x 50 Free on :50
Cool down:	200
Total:	4,900

43 Workout

Challenge: Focus and refocus on your pace as often as necessary.

Warm up:	500
Kick:	400 IM
Drill/Swim:	12 x 50 w/15 SR – alternating 25s of your favorite Drill/Swim
Swim:	400 Free, 100 IM, 300 Free, 200 IM, 200 Free, 300 IM, 100 Free, 400 IM w/:30 SR
100 Easy	
Kick:	200 Choice
Pull:	200
Swim:	8 x 50 on :45 – alternating 25s of Stroke Specialty/Free
Swim:	8 x 50 on :45 – alternating 50s of Stroke Specialty/Free
Cool down:	200
Total:	5,000

44 Workout

Challenge: Smile during every rest.

Warm up:	500
Kick:	400 Choice
Drill:	400 IM order – your favorite Drills
Pull:	500

Swim:	5 x 100 Free on 1:30
Swim:	6 x 200 on 3:00 – odd lengths IM order, even lengths Free

100 Easy

Kick:	500 w/Fins – streamline position
Swim:	4 x 25 Fly on :30
Swim:	4 x 25 Back on :30
Swim:	4 x 25 Breast on :30
Swim:	4 x 25 Free on :30
Swim:	2 x 25 Fly on :30
Swim:	2 x 25 Back on :30
Swim:	2 x 25 Breast on :30
Swim:	2 x 25 Free on :30
Swim:	1 x 25 Fly on :30
Swim:	1 x 25 Back on :30
Swim:	1 x 25 Breast on :30
Swim:	x 25 Free on :30

Cool down:	200
Total:	5,000

45 Workout

Challenge: Visualize the performance of a lifetime.

Warm up:	500
Kick:	400 IM
Drill:	400 IM – your favorite Drills
Swim:	10 x 100 Free on 1:30
Swim:	10 x 100 Stroke Specialty on 1:40
100 Easy	
Kick:	500 w/Fins – streamline position
Swim:	8 x 50 Free on :45
Swim:	8 x 50 Worst Stroke on 1:00
100 Easy	
Swim:	8 x 25 on :30 – alternating 25s Stroke Specialty/ Worst Stroke
Cool down:	200
Total:	5,200

Workout 46

Challenge: How does versatility bring you closer to your goal?

Warm up:	500
Kick:	200 Flutter
Kick:	200 Choice
Drill:	200 your favorite Stroke Specialty Drill
Drill:	200 your favorite weak stroke Drill
Swim:	6 x 150 Free on 2:15 – at your 100 pace
100 Easy	
Swim:	6 x 100 Stroke Specialty w/15 SR
Swim:	5 x 100 2nd Stroke Specialty w/15 SR
Swim:	4 x 100 3rd Stroke Specialty w/15 SR
Swim:	3 x 100 4th Stroke Specialty w/15 SR
100 Easy	
Kick:	200 Choice
Pull:	500 – Breathing Sequence: by 25 – every 3, 5, 7, 9...
Kick:	8 x 25 on :40 – alternating 25s of Flutter/Stroke Specialty Kick
Cool down:	200
Total:	5,300

47 Workout

Challenge: Say to yourself, "IM is the triathlon of swimming, and I am an Iron Man!"

Warm up:	500
Kick:	300 Choice
Drill:	400 IM order – your favorite Alignment Drills
Swim:	4 x 250 IM w/30 SR – double Fly
Swim:	4 x 250 IM w/30 SR – double Back
Swim:	4 x 250 IM w/30 SR – double Breast
Swim:	4 x 250 IM w/30 SR – double Free
Cool down:	200
Total:	5,400

48 Workout

Challenge: Concentrate on your IM through its parts.

Warm up:	500
Kick:	500 Choice – alternating 25s of two different kicks
Drill:	400 IM Drill – your favorite Leverage Drills
Swim:	4 x 100 Free on 1:30 – Descending
Swim:	8 x 200 w/:20 SR – Free, Stroke Specialty, Worst Stroke, IM...
100 Easy	
Kick:	4 x 100 on 1:30 w/Fins – streamline position
Pull:	500 – Breathing Sequence: by 25 – every 3, 5, 7, 9...
100 Easy	
Kick:	4 x 25 Fly on :30
Swim:	4 x 50 Free on :45
Kick:	4 x 25 Back on :30
Swim:	4 x 50 Free on :45
Kick:	4 x 25 Breast on :30
Swim:	4 x 50 Free on :45
Kick:	4 x 25 Free on :30
Cool down:	200
Total:	5,700

Workout

Challenge: Mobilize for any distance IM.

Warm up:	500
Kick/Swim:	20 x 50 on 1:00 – alternating 50s of Flutter Kick/Free
Drill/Swim:	4 x 100 w/15 SR – IM order, alternating 25s of your favorite Feel Drills/Swim
Swim:	2 x 400 IM w/60 SR
100 Easy	
Swim:	4 x 200 IM w/30 SR
100 Easy	
Swim:	8 x 100 IM w/20 SR
100 Easy	
Kick:	200 Choice
Kick:	200 w/Fins – streamline position
Pull:	500
Cool down:	200
Total:	5,700

50 Workout

Challenge: Visualize building through each stroke.

Warm up:	500
Kick/Swim:	8 x 50 on 1:00 – alternating 50s of Flutter Kick/ Freestyle
Drill/Swim:	4 x 100 w/15 SR – alternating 25s of your favorite Coordination Drills/Swim
Swim:	10 x 150 Free on 2:15
Swim:	0 x 150 IM without Free on 2:30
100 Easy	
Kick:	4 x 100 w/Fins on 1:30 – streamline position
Pull:	400
Swim:	8 x 25 Stroke Specialty on :30
Kick:	8 x 25 Choice on :40
Swim:	8 x 25 Free on :30
Cool down:	200
Total:	6,000

SPRINT WORKOUTS

The following workouts are appropriate for sprint training. Contents include race pace and threshold work, speed play, broken swimming and degree of effort work. Swim distances range from 25 to 500 yards/meters. Set distances range from 200 to 1,000 yards/meters. Workouts distances range from 4,000 to 4,600 yards/meters. Workouts in this section are smaller in volume but greater in intensity the in the other sections of this book. More rest than normal is recommended between sets. More recovery time is recommended between workouts. Warm up and cool down distances are shown as the minimum distance recommended.

Approach each workout with three goals:

1. Make the most of each workout challenge presented throughout the session by mentally engaging in goal affirmation, positive self-talk, focusing on the task at hand, controlling adapting and visualizing.

2. Perform each workout with effort that challenges your fitness level, and quality that reinforces for swimming efficiency.

3. Have fun with it!

51 Workout

Challenge: Reaching your goal requires knowing your degree of effort.

Warm up:	500
Kick:	300 Flutter
Drill:	300 your favorite Feel Drill
Swim:	8 x 25 – Build on :30
Swim:	5 x 100 Freestyle on 1:30 – 85 % Pace
100 Easy	
Swim:	5 x 100 Freestyle on 1:30 – Descending 85% – 100%
100 Easy	
Kick:	200 Choice
Drill:	200 your favorite Coordination Drill
Swim:	4 x 50 Free on 1:00 – 80% Effort
Kick:	4 x 50 Flutter w/15 SR
Swim:	4 x 50 Free on 1:30 – 90% Effort
Kick:	4 x 50 Flutter w/15 SR
Swim:	4 x 50 Free on 3:00 – 100% Effort
Cool down:	200
Total:	4,000

52 Workout

Challenge: Say to yourself, "Fast is fun!"

Warm up:	500
Kick:	200 Flutter
Drill:	300 your favorite Alignment Drill
Kick:	200 Choice
Drill:	300 your favorite Feel Drill
Swim:	8 x 75 Free – Build w/20 SR
100 Easy	
Swim:	8 x 75 Free – Middle length Fast w/20 SR
100 Easy	
Swim:	8 x 75 Free – 50 Fast, 25 Easy
100 Easy	
Kick:	8 x 25 Stroke Specialty w/15 SR – odd 25s Easy, even 25s Fast
Cool down:	200
Total:	4,000

Workout

Challenge: Focus on your pace.

Warm up:	500
Kick:	8 x 50 Flutter on 1:00
Drill/Swim:	3 x 200 – alternating 25s of your favorite Drills/Swim
Swim:	12 x 100 on 1:30 – every third 100 is Non-free
100 Easy	
Pull:	500
Swim:	4 x 25 Free on :45 – add up total swim time
100 Easy	
Swim:	2 x 50 Free on 1:15 – add up total swim time – beat total time of 4 x 25
100 Easy	
Swim:	100 Free – beat total time of 2 x 50
Cool down:	200
Total:	4,000

54 Workout

Challenge: How would you respond positively to team pressure to score a win?

Warm up:	500
Kick:	300 Flutter
Drill/Swim:	4 x 100 – alternating 50s of your favorite Leverage Drill/Swim w/15 SR
Swim:	4 x 100 on 1:45 – Descending
100 Easy	
Swim:	4 x 100 on 1:45 – Descending from third 100 above
100 Easy	
Swim:	4 x 100 on 1:45 – Descending from third 100 above
100 Easy	
Kick:	200 Choice
Pull:	500
100 Easy	
Swim:	12 x 25 Choice on :45 – odd 25s Fast, even 25s Easy
Cool down:	200
Total:	4,000

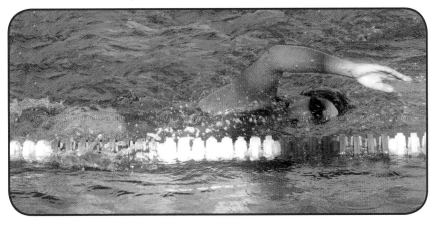

55 Workout

Challenge: Visualize perfect pace.

Warm up:	500
Kick:	500 Flutter
Drill:	8 x 50 – your favorite Drills w/:15 SR
Swim:	12 x 50 Free on 1:00 – calculate average time
100 Easy	
Swim:	6 x 100 on Free 2:00 – calculate average time, divide by 2 – should equal to average 50 time above
100 Easy	
Swim:	3 x 200 Free on 4:00 – calculate average time, divide by 4 – should equal to average 50 time above
100 Easy	
Kick:	200 Choice
Swim:	4 x 25 Choice on 1:00 at 100%
Cool down:	200
Total:	4,000

56 Workout

Challenge: State your goal with conviction.

Warm up:	500
Kick:	300 – 50 medium, 25 fast
Drill/Swim:	3 x 200 – your favorite Alignment drills w/20 SR
Swim:	8 x 75 w/:15 SR – middle length Non-free
Swim:	4 x 200 Free on 3:15

1. First 50 Fast
2. 2nd 50 Fast
3. 3rd 50 Fast
4. Last 50 Fast

100 Easy

Kick:	300 Choice
Pull:	5 x 100 on 1:30
Swim:	2 x 25 Choice – Fast w/30 SR
Swim:	50 Easy
Swim:	2 x 25 Choice – Fast w/30 SR
Swim:	50 Easy
Swim:	2 x 25 Choice – Fast w/30 SR
Swim:	50 Easy
Swim:	2 x 25 Choice – Fast w/30 SR
Swim:	50 Easy
Cool down:	200
Total:	4,000

57 Workout

Challenge: Say to yourself, "I love to sprint."

Warm up:	500
Kick:	10 x 50 Flutter or Dolphin on 1:00
Drill/Swim:	4 x 200 – alternating 25s of your favorite Drills/ Swim w/20 SR
Swim:	6 x 100 Free on 1:40 – timed
100 Easy	
Swim:	5 x 100 Free on 1:35 – match best time above
100 Easy	
Swim:	4 x 100 Free on 1:30 – match best time above
100 Easy	
Kick:	8 x 25 w/Fins – streamline position on :30
Cool down:	200
Total:	4,000

Workout 58

Challenge: Summon your sprint on demand.

Warm up:	500
Kick/Drill:	10 x 100 alternating 100s of Flutter/your favorite Drills
Swim:	200 Free at 80% w/2:00 rest
Swim:	50 Choice at 100% w/2:00 rest
Swim:	200 Free at 80% w/2:00 rest
Swim:	50 Choice at 100% w/2:00 rest
Swim:	200 Free at 80% w/2:00 rest
Swim:	50 Choice at 100% w/2:00 rest
Swim:	200 Free at 80% w/2:00 rest
Swim:	50 Choice at 100%
100 Easy	
Kick:	200 Choice
Pull:	500
Kick/Swim:	8 x 50 – alternating 50s of Choice Kick/Choice Swim on 1:00

50 Easy

Swim:	50 choice at 100% – try for best time of the day
Cool down:	200
Total:	4,000

Workout

Challenge: How would you respond positively to a freezing swim meet morning?

Warm up:	500
Kick/Drill:	10 x 100 alternating 100s of Flutter/your favorite Drills
Swim:	4 x 200 – alternating 25s of Free/Non-Free on 3:15
Swim:	4 x 100 on 1:30 – Breathing every 5 strokes
100 Easy	
Pull:	500 – Breathing Sequence: by 25 – every 3, 5, 7, 9...
100 Easy	
Swim:	8 x 50 on 1:00 – odd 50s Fast, even 50s Easy
Cool down:	200
Total:	4,000

61 Workout

Challenge: Visualize knowing that you are swimming your best time.

Warm up:	500
Kick:	400 flutter or Dolphin
Drill:	300 your favorite Feel Drill
Swim:	8 x 75 – Build w/15 SR
Swim:	8 x 75 – Descending w/15 SR
Pull:	500
Swim:	12 x 50 on 1:00 – Predict your time on even 50s
100 Easy	
Kick:	8 x 25 Kick on :40 – Predict your time on even 25s
Cool down:	200
Total:	4,000

Workout

Challenge: Achieving your goal means reaching past the comfort zone.

Warm up:	500
Kick:	8 x 50 Flutter or Dolphin on 1:00
Drill/Swim:	4 x 100 – alternating 25s of your favorite Alignment Drills/Swim w/20 SR
Swim:	12 x 75 – Build w/:15 SR
Swim:	4 x Broken 200 Free w/1:00 rest:
	1 & 3: 1 x 100 + 4 x 25 w/10 SR – (Note total time -40 sec)
	2 & 4: 4 x 25 + 1 x 100 w/10 SR – (Note total time -40 sec)
100 Easy	
Kick:	200 Choice
Pull:	400
Swim:	200 Free for time – Try to match best broken 200 time above
Cool down:	200
Total:	4,100

Workout

Challenge: Say to yourself, "I am stronger than ever before."

Warm up:	500
Kick:	300 Flutter or Dolphin
Drill/Swim:	4 x 200 – alternating 50s of your favorite Leverage Drill/Swim w/20 SR
Kick:	8 x 50 w/Fins on :30 – streamline position
Swim:	10 x 50 – Build on :1:00
Swim:	6 x Broken 100 Free w/60 SR:
	1 & 4: 2 x 50 w/:20 SR (Note total time -20 sec)
	2 & 5: 1 x 50 + 2 x 25 w/:10 SR (Note total time -20 sec)
	3 & 6: 2 x 25 + 1 x 50 w/:10 SR (Note total time -20 sec)
100 Easy	
Kick:	200 Choice
Pull:	500

Swim:	100 Free for time – Try to match best broken 100 time above
Cool down:	200
Total:	4,100

Workout

Challenge: How would you eliminate distractions before your event?

Warm up:	500
Kick:	10 x 50 Flutter on 1:00
Drill:	6 x 100 – your favorite Drills w/20 SR
Swim:	5 x 100 Free on 1:30
Swim:	8 x 50 Free w/2:00 resl:
	Odd 50s: 2 x 25 w/20 SR (Note total time -20 sec)
	Even 50s: 50 Fast – Match Broken 50 times
100 Easy	
Kick:	300 Choice
Pull:	500
Kick:	400 w/Fins – streamline position
Swim:	50 Free for time – Try to match best 50 time above
Cool down:	200
Total:	4,150

Workout 64

Challenge: How would you respond positively if you are feeling jet lagged and your event is in an hour?

Warm up:	500
Kick:	8 x 50 Flutter or Dolphin on 1:00
Drill/Swim:	8 x 100 – alternating 50s of your favorite Drills/Swim w/:0 SR
Swim:	4 x 25 Free w/:30 SR – Build
Swim:	4 x 25 Free w/:30 SR – Half length at 100%, half length Easy
Swim:	4 x 25 Free w/:30 SR – Half length, Easy, half length at 100%
Swim:	4 x 25 Free w/:30 SR – Fast
100 Easy	
Kick:	200 Choice
Kick:	8 x 50 w/Fins – streamline position on :45
Pull:	400
Swim:	200 Choice w/1:00 rest
Swim:	50 Free for time w/1:00 rest

Swim:	200 Choice w/1:00 rest
Swim:	50 Free for time w/1:00 rest
Swim:	200 Choice w/1:00 rest
Swim:	50 Free for time – Best of the Day
Cool down:	200
Total:	4,250

65 Workout

Challenge: Visualize precision swimming.

Warm up:	500
Kick:	8 x 50 Flutter or Dolphin on 1:00
Drill/Swim:	8 x 50 – alternating 50s of your favorite Drills/Swim w/15 SR
Swim:	3 x 200 Free – Descending on 4:00 (at 80, 90, 100%)
100 Easy	
Swim:	5 x 100 Free – Descending on 2:00 (at 80, 85, 90, 95, 100%)
100 Easy	
Swim:	8 x 50 Free – Descending on 1:00 (2 each at 85, 90, 95, 100%)
100 Easy	
Kick:	500 w/Fins – streamline position
Pull:	300
Swim:	8 x 25 Free on 1:00 – odd 25s at 80%, even 25s at 100%
Cool down:	200
Total:	4,300

Workout

Challenge: Affirm that you are doing what it takes to reach your goal.

Warm up:	500
Kick:	400 Flutter or Dolphin
Drill/Swim:	6 x 100 w/20 SR – 75 your favorite Drills/25 Swim
Swim:	3 x 200 Free on 3:15
Swim:	2 x 200 Free on 3:15 – no breathing in and out of the flags
100 Easy	
Pull:	500 – Breathing Sequence: by 25 – every 3, 5, 7, 9 …
Swim:	3 x 100 Free on 1:30
Swim:	2 x 100 Free on 1:30 – no breathing in and out of the flags
100 Easy	

Kick:	200
Swim:	8 x 25 Fast Free on 1:00
	1 & 5: 3 breaths
	2 & 6: 2 breaths
	3 & 7: 1 breath
	4 & 8: 0 breaths
Cool down:	200
Total:	4,300

67 Workout

Challenge: Say to yourself, "I can go faster than ever before."

Warm up:	500
Kick:	300 Flutter or Dolphin
Drill/Swim:	300 – alternating 50s of your favorite Alignment Drill/Swim
Swim:	8 x 100 Free on 1:30 – Descend 1 – 4 & 5 – 8
100 Easy	
Drill/Swim:	300 – alternating 50s of your favorite Leverage Drill/Swim
Swim:	100 Free for time
100 Easy	
Swim:	10 x 50 Free on :45 – Descend 1 – 5 & 6 – 10
100 Easy	
Drill/Swim:	300 – alternating 50s of your favorite Feel Drill/Swim
Swim:	50 Free for time
100 Easy	
Swim:	12 x 25 Free on :30 – Descend 1 – 4, 5 – 8, & 9 – 12
100 Easy	
Drill/Swim:	300 – alternating 50s of your favorite Feel Drill/Swim
Swim:	25 Free for time
Cool down:	200
Total:	4,375

Workout

Challenge: Apply your speed to free and non-free.

Warm up:	500
Kick: 200	Flutter or Dolphin
Drill/Swim:	300 – alternating 50s of your favorite Free Drills/Swim
Drill/Swim:	300 – alternating 50s of your favorite Non-free Drills/Swim
Swim:	8 x 100 on 1:45 – alternating 100s of Non-free/Free
100 Easy	
Kick:	400 w/Fins – streamline position
Swim:	8 x 50 – on 2:00 – alternating 50s of 100% Free/80% Non-free
100 Easy	
Kick:	200 Choice
Pull:	400
Swim:	8 x 50 – on 2:00 – alternating 50s of 100% Non-Free/80% Free
Cool down:	200
Total:	4,400

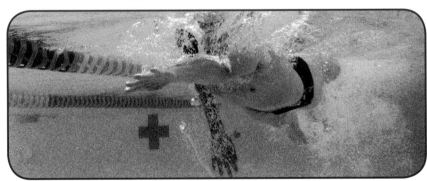

69 Workout

Challenge: Adapt to the demands of each swim, as you must on race day.

Warm up:	500
Kick:	300 Flutter or Dolphin
Drill:	200 – your favorite Stroke Path Drill
Kick:	300 w/Fins – streamline position

Swim:	4 x 100 Free – Build on 1:40 – note times
Swim:	4 x 100 Free – Descending on 1:40 – match times above

100 Easy

Swim:	4 x 50 Free – Build on :50 – note times
Swim:	4 x 50 Free – Descending on :50 – match times above

100 Easy

Swim:	4 x 100 Free – Build on 1:30 – note times
Swim:	4 x 100 Free – Descending on 1:30 – match times above

100 Easy

Swim:	4 x 50 Free – Build on :45 – note times
Swim:	4 x 50 Free – Descending on :45 – match times above

Cool down:	200
Total:	4,400

70 Workout

Challenge: Visualize race pace with all of your senses.

Warm up:	500
Kick:	300 – alternating 25s of Flutter or Dolphin
Drill:	4 x 200 – alternating 50s of your favorite Drills/Swim
Swim:	4 x 50 Free – Build
Swim:	200 Free – long and loose
Swim:	4 x 50 Free – 25 Fast/25 Easy
Swim:	200 long and loose
Swim:	4 x 50 Descending
Swim:	200 long and loose
Swim:	4 x 50 Burst – each 25 is half fast/half easy
100 Easy	

Kick:	400
Pull:	400
Swim:	1 x 50 Free w/Fins – note time
100 Easy	
Kick:	1 x 50 Flutter w/Fins – match swim time above
100 Easy	
Swim:	1 x 50 Free at 100% – match swim time w/ Fins
Cool down:	200
Total:	4,450

71 Workout

Challenge: Own your goal pace.

Warm up:	500
Kick/Swim:	12 x 50 – alternating 25s of Flutter or Dolphin/ Swim on 1:00
Drill/Swim:	8 x 100 – alternating 50s of your favorite Drills/ Swim w/15 SR
Divide Goal:	100 time by 4
	Swim: 4 x 25 on 1:00 at that rate
	Swim: 4 x 25 on :55 at that rate
	Swim: 4 x 25 on :50 at that rate
100 Easy	
Kick:	300 Choice
Pull:	500
Divide Goal:	100 time by 2
	Swim: 2 x 50 on 2:00 at that rate
	Swim: 2 x 50 on 1:45 at that rate
	Swim: 2 x 50 on 1:30 at that rate
100 Easy	
Kick:	300 Choice
Pull:	500
Cool down:	200
Total:	4,500

72 Workout

Challenge: Say to yourself, "I am ready to do my best time."

Warm up:	500
Kick:	8 x 50 Flutter or Dolphin on 1:00
Drill/Swim:	3 x 200 – alternating 50s of your favorite Drills/ Swim
Divide Best:	200 time by 8
	Swim: 8 x 25 on 1:00 at that rate
	Swim: 8 x 25 on :55 at that rate
	Swim: 8 x 25 on :50 at that rate
100 Easy	
Kick:	200 Choice
Pull:	200
Divide Best:	200 time by 4
	Swim: 4 x 50 on 2:00 at that rate
	Swim: 4 x 50 on 1:45 at that rate
	Swim: 4 x 50 on 1:30 at that rate
100 Easy	
Kick:	200 Choice
Pull:	200

Divide Best:	200 time by 2
	Swim: 2 x 100 on 4:00 at that rate
	Swim: 2 x 100 on 3:30 at that rate
	Swim: 2 x 100 on 3:00 at that rate
Cool down:	200
Total:	4,600

73 Workout

Challenge: Mentally prepare to swim at 100%.

Warm up:	500
Kick:	200 Flutter or Dolphin
Drill:	200 – your favorite Drill
Kick:	200 w/Fins
Drill/Swim:	200 – alternating 25s of your favorite Drill/Swim
Swim:	4 x 50 Free on :45
Swim:	4 x 75 Free w/20 SR – at your 50 rate
100 Easy	
Swim:	100 for time
100 Easy	
Swim:	4 x 50 Free on :45
Swim:	4 x 75 Free w/20 SR – at your 50 rate
100 Easy	
Swim:	100 for time
100 Easy	
Swim:	4 x 50 Free on :45
Swim:	4 x 75 Free w/20 SR – at your 50 rate
100 Easy	
Swim:	100 for time
100 Easy	
Swim:	4 x 50 Free on :45
Swim:	4 x 75 Free w/20 SR – at your 50 rate
100 Easy	
Swim:	100 for time – Best of the day
Cool down:	200
Total:	4,600

74 Workout

Challenge: How would you respond positively to being seeded in a slow heat?

Warm up:	500
Kick:	200 Flutter
Kick:	200 Dolphin
Drill:	200 your favorite
Kick:	200 w/Fins – streamline position
Swim:	8 x 100 Free on 1:30
100 Easy	
Swim:	8 x 50 Free on 1:00 – Bursts
	Each is 25 + Turn Fast, the rest Easy
100 Easy	
Pull:	400
Swim:	8 x 50 Free on 1:30 – Bursts
	Each 25 is half Fast, half Easy
100 Easy	
Kick:	400 Choice

Swim:	8 x 50 Free on 2:00 – Bursts
	1 & 5: 12 Fast strokes, then the rest Easy
	2 & 6: 10 Fast strokes, then the rest Easy
	3 & 7: 8 Fast strokes, then the rest Easy
	4 & 8: 6 Fast strokes, then the rest Easy
Cool down:	200
Total:	4,600

75 Workout

Challenge: Visualize an amazing finish.

Warm up:	500
Kick:	200 Flutter or Dolphin
Drill/Swim:	4 x 100 – alternating 50s of your favorite Drills/ Swim w/20 SR
Swim:	8 x 75 w/:15 SR – rotate through 25 Fast
Swim:	2 x 400 Broken Free w/60 SR
	1: 200 + 4 x 50 w/:15 SR (note total time -1 min)
	2: 4 x 50 + 200 w/:15 SR (note total time -1 min)
100 Easy	
Swim:	2 x 400 Broken Free w/60 SR
	1: 200 + 2 x 100 w/:20 SR (note total time -1 min)
	2: 2 x 100 + 200 w/:20 SR (note total time -1 min)
100 Easy	
Kick:	200
Pull:	300
Swim:	400 Free – Try to match best 400 time above
Cool down:	200
Total:	4,600

DISTANCE WORKOUTS

The following workouts are appropriate for distance and open water swimming workouts and for triathletes. Contents include general endurance, pace work, timed distance swimming and interval work. Swim distances range from 50 to 3,000 yards/meters. Set distances range from 500 to 3,000 yards/meters. Workouts distances range from 4,400 to 6,000 yards/meters. Warm up and Cool down distances are shown as the minimum distance recommended.

Approach each workout with three goals:

1. Make the most of each workout challenge presented throughout the session by mentally engaging in goal affirmation, positive self-talk, focusing on the task at hand, controlling, adapting and visualizing.

2. Perform each workout with effort that challenges your fitness level, and quality that reinforces for swimming efficiency.

3. Have fun with it!

Workout

Challenge: Know your goal pace.

Warm up:	800
Kick:	400 Flutter
Drill/Swim:	500 – alternating 50 – your favorite Leverage Drill/Free
Swim/Pull:	10 x 100 – alternating 100 of Free/Pull – Breathing Sequence: by 25 – every 3, 5, 7, 9 ...
Swim:	100, 200, 300, 400, 500, 400, 300, 200, 100 w/30 SR
Cool down:	200
Total:	4,400

77 Workout

Challenge: Choose a power word and repeat it to yourself to stay on pace.

Warm up:	800
Kick:	8 x 50 Flutter on 1:00
Drill:	4 x 100 – alternating 25s of your favorite Stroke Path Drill/Swim w/20 SR
Swim:	4 x 500 on 7:00
100 Easy	
Swim:	10 x 50 Free on :45
Cool down:	200
Total:	4,400

Workout

Challenge: Maintain your focus ... count accurately!

Warm up:	800
Kick:	300 Flutter
Drill:	300 – your favorite Leverage Drill
Swim:	3,000 for time
Cool down:	200
Total:	4,600

79 Workout

Challenge: Overcome the urge to daydream ... stay focused on maintaining your pace.

Warm up:	800
Kick:	200 Flutter
Kick:	200 w/Fins – streamline position
Swim:	10 x 50 w/:10 SR, then Fast 500 – note total time -50 sec
100 Easy	
Swim:	5 x 100 Free w/15 SR, then 500 Fast – note total time -75 sec
100 Easy	
Swim:	1000 – compare times to above
Cool down:	200
Total:	4,600

Workout

Challenge: Visualize yourself using the water effectively and moving forward with ease.

Warm up:	800
Kick:	200 Flutter
Kick:	300 w/Fins – streamline position
Drill/Swim:	400 – your favorite Coordination Drill
Swim/Kick:	1,000 – alternating 75 Swim/25 Kick
100 Easy	
Swim/Kick:	6 x 200 w/20 SR – alternating 200s of Kick/Swim
100 Easy	
Pull:	500 – Breathing Sequence: by 25 – every 3, 5, 7, 9 ...
Cool down:	200
Total:	4,700

84 Workout

Challenge: Assert your commitment to your goal with every flip turn.

Warm up:	800
Kick:	300 Flutter
Drill:	300 – your favorite Alignment Drill
Kick:	300 w/Fins – streamline position
Swim:	20 x 50 + 500 on :45
100 Easy	
Swim:	500 w/30 SR + 20 x 50 on :45
Cool down:	200
Total:	4,800

Workout

Challenge: Say to yourself, "I can hold my pace to the finish."

Warm up:	800
Kick:	200 Flutter
Drill:	200 – your favorite Alignment Drill
Kick:	200 Flutter
Drill:	200 – your favorite Leverage Drill
Swim:	5 x 100 Free on 1:30, then 500 Fast – note total time
100 Easy	
Swim:	5 x 100 Free on 1:30, then 500 Fast – compare total time to above
100 Easy	
Swim:	5 x 100 Free on 1:30, then 500 Fast – compare total time to above
Cool down:	200
Total:	5,000

83 Workout

Challenge: Practice channeling your energy into the each swim.

Warm up:	800
Kick:	4 x 100 Flutter w/15 SR
Drill/Swim:	6 x 100 w/:15 SR – alternating 25s of your favorite Drills
Swim:	10 x 100 on 1:30 – Descend 1 – 5 & 6 – 10 (Keep all 100s within a 15 sec. range)
100 Easy	
Swim:	1,000
100 Easy	
Swim:	5 x 200 on 3:00 – Descending (Keep all 200s within a 15 sec. range)
Cool down:	200
Total:	5,000

84 Workout

Challenge: How would you respond positively if the water was choppy?

Warm up:	800
Kick:	200 Flutter
Swim:	5 x 100 on 1:30 – Pace
Swim:	4 x 500 on 7:00 – Descending
100 Easy	
Kick:	200
Swim:	2 x 500 on 7:00 – Descend from best time above
Cool down:	200
Total:	5,200

85 Workout

Challenge: Visualize knowing the 1,000 like the back of your hand.

Warm up:	800
Kick:	200 Flutter
Drill/Swim:	300 – your favorite Stroke Path Drill
Pull:	500
Swim:	800 Pace + 8 x 25 Fast w/30 SR
100 Easy	
Swim:	800 Pace + 4 x 50 Fast w/30 SR
100 Easy	
Swim:	800 Pace + 2 x 100 Fast w/30 SR
Cool down:	200
Total:	5,200

Workout

Challenge: Keep your goal clearly in mind as it gets tough.

Warm up:	800
Kick:	10 x 50 Flutter on 1:00
Drill:	400 – alternating 50s of your favorite Leverage Drill
Kick:	400 w/Fins – streamline position
Swim:	10 x 100 on 1:30
Swim:	8 x 100 on 1:25
Swim:	6 x 100 on 1:20
Swim:	4 x 100 on 1:15
Swim:	2 x 100 on 1:10
Cool down:	200
Total:	5,300

87 Workout

Challenge: Say to yourself, "I am ready to go for it."

Warm up:	800
Kick:	4 x 50 Flutter on 1:00
Kick:	200 w/Fins
Kick:	4 x 50 on 1:00
Drill:	4 x 100 – alternating 50s of your favorite Coordination Drills/Free w15 SR
Swim:	10 x 200 – 10 SR after odd 200s, 20 SR after even 200s
100 Easy	
Kick:	300
Swim:	10 x 100 – 10 SR after odd 100s, 15 SR after even 100s
Cool down:	200
Total:	5,400

Workout

Challenge: Focus on your own race.

Warm up:	800
Kick/Drill:	500 – alternating 50s of Flutter/your favorite Drill
Swim:	20 x 50 on :45
Swim:	3,000 for time – compare time with Workout #77
Cool down:	200
Total:	5,500

89 Workout

Challenge: How would you ensure enough sleep and a good diet at an away meet?

Warm up:	800
Kick:	4 x 200 – alternating 200s without/with Fins w/30 SR
Drill/Swim:	4 x 200 – alternating 50s of your favorite Drills/Free
Swim:	400 for time
Swim:	5 x 400 w/45 SR
100 Easy	
Swim:	400 for time – Best of the Day
Cool down:	200
Total:	5,500

90 Workout

Challenge: Visualize yourself moving through the water effortlessly.

Warm up:	800
Kick:	8 x 50 Flutter on 1:00
Drill/Swim:	300 your favorite Drill/Free
Swim:	10 x 100 on 1:30
Swim:	200 for time
100 Easy	
Swim:	10 x 100 on 1:30
Swim:	200 for time
100 Easy	
Swim:	10 x 100 on 1:30
Swim:	200 for time
100 Easy	
Cool down:	200
Total:	5,600

91 Workout

Challenge: Count out the seconds you need to shave to reach your goal.

Warm up:	800
Kick:	200
Drill:	300
Kick:	400 w/Fins
Drill/Swim:	500 – alternating 50s of your favorite Drill/Free
Swim:	5 x 100 on 1:30 – 1st 100 Fastest
Swim:	5 x 100 on 1:30 – 2nd 100 Fastest
Swim:	5 x 100 on 1:30 – 3rd 100 Fastest
Swim:	5 x 100 on 1:30 – 4th 100 Fastest
Swim:	5 x 100 on 1:30 – 5th 100 Fastest
100 Easy	
Kick:	200
Swim:	500 for time
Cool down:	200
Total:	5,700

Workout

Challenge: Choose three "power words" to energize you.

Warm up:	800
Kick:	400 – 25 Fast/25 Easy
Drill:	400 – alternating 50s of your favorite Drill/Free
Swim:	16 x 50 on :45
Swim:	8 x 100 on 1:30
Swim:	4 x 200 on 3:00
Swim:	2 x 400 on 6:00
Swim:	800 for time
Cool down:	200
Total:	5,800

93 Workout

Challenge: Keep your eye on the prize!

Warm up: 800
Kick: 5 x 100 Flutter w/15 SR

Swim: 500, 1,000, 1,500, 1,000, 500 w/60 SR

Cool down: 200
Total: 6,000

94 Workout

Challenge: Practice re-establishing your pace.

Warm up:	800
Kick:	8 x 50 Flutter on 1:00
Drill:	200 – your favorite Alignment Drill
Drill/Swim:	8 x 50 – alternating 25s of your favorite Drill/Free
Swim:	4 x 1,000 w/60 SR

1. Every 4th length Non-free
2. All Free
3. 50 Free, 50 Non-free
4. All Free

Cool down:	200
Total:	6,000

95 Workout

Challenge: Visualize ultimate stroke efficiency.

Warm up:	800
Kick:	400 Flutter
Drill/Swim:	12 x 50 – alternating 25s of your favorite Drills/ Free
Swim:	40 x 100 on 1:20
Cool down:	200
Total:	6,000

96 Workout

Challenge: Own your goal by swimming one second faster per 100.

Warm up:	800
Kick:	10 x 50 Flutter on 1:00
Kick:	400 w/Fins – streamline position
Swim:	500 + 5 x 100 Descending on 1:20
Swim:	500 + 10 x 50 Descending on :40
100 Easy	
Swim:	500 + 5 x 100 Descending on 1:20
Swim:	500 + 10 x 50 Descending on :40
Cool down:	200
Total:	6,000

97 Workout

Challenge: Say to yourself, "I am physically and mentally prepared."

Warm up:	800
Kick:	300 Flutter
Drill:	200 – your favorite Drill
Kick:	300 w/Fins – streamline position
Drill/Swim:	200 – alternating 25s of your favorite Drill/Free
Swim:	4 x 250 – Odd lengths Breath every 3 strokes
100 Easy	

Swim:	Swim: 4 x 250 – Odd lengths Breath every 5 strokes
100 Easy	
Swim:	4 x 250 – Odd lengths Breath every 7 strokes
100 Easy	
Swim:	4 x 250 – Odd lengths Breath every 9 strokes
Cool down:	200
Total:	6,000

98 Workout

Challenge: What is your strategy to achieve your best 3,000 time?

Warm up: 800

3,000 for time – compare time with Workout #77 & #87

Cool down: 200
Total: 6,000

Workout

Challenge: How would you positively respond to feeling sluggish before your race?

Warm up:	800
Swim:	10 x 500 on 7:00
Cool down:	200
Total:	6,000

156

Workout

Challenge: Visualize endless energy.

Warm up:	800
Kick:	500 Flutter – alternating 25s of Fast/Easy
Drill/Swim:	10 x 50 – alternating 25s of your favorite Drills/ Free w/15 SR

Swim:	4 x 1,000 with :60 SR
	1. 75 Fast/25 Easy
	2. 50 Fast/50 Easy
	3. 25 Fast/75 Easy
	4. All Fast

Cool down:	200
Total:	6,000

CONCLUSION

It is my hope that as you worked your way through these workouts, you have felt yourself become stronger, faster, more focused, and more mentally prepared to do your best in competition. By working on training your mind as well as your body, you have risen to a new level of development. Take time to do another self-interview, with the questions on page 18. Notice how you have evolved.

I hope you have had fun challenging your body and your mind! I hope that you are motivated to reach higher than ever with your swimming.

Now, go for it!

CREDITS

Cover design: Sabine Groten

Cover photos: dpa Picture-Alliance GmbH; © Fotolia.com

Illustrations by: Blythe Lucero

Photography: Steve Sturges, Avital Brodin, Blythe Lucero

Swimmers appearing in the photos: Vicky Augustine, Jennifer Barra, Pam Bennett, Conny Bleul-Gohlke, Jonas Brodin, Kathryn Cohen, Monique Comacchio, Saio Costantino, Lessley Field, Annie Fujimoto, Seth Goddard, Liam Godfrey, Bill Grant, Katie Grue, Caroline Howard, Laura Howard, Eric Johnson, Blythe Lucero, Elise Lusk, Karen Matsuoka, Kim O'Keefe, Alvaro Pastor, Alissa Perrucchi, Ida Price, Juliana Price, Eric Rhodes, Dave Robert, Matt Snyderman, Lissa Suden, Jack Tomasik, Tom Trauger, Spencer Tuma, Michael Woodruff

Swim to the Top

Blythe Lucero
The 100 Best Swimming Drills

Swimming drills allow a swimmer to concentrate on a single aspect of a stroke at one time. The book is organized into sections covering the four competitive strokes: freestyle, backstroke, breaststroke and butterfly. Each drill is explained step-by-step and accompanied by comprehensive diagrams. Drill feedback charts are included to help swimmers identify problems and make modifications. Underwater and surface photographs give swimmers optimal images to emulate as they practice.

2nd edition
280 pages, full-color print
132 color photos,
135 illustrations, 100 charts
Paperback, 6^1/2" x 9^1/4"
ISBN: 9781841262161
$ 19.95 US / $ 32.95 AUS
£ 14.95 UK/€ 19.95

Lucero/Bleul-Gohlke
Masters Swimming – A Manual

Masters Swimming – A Manual lets every reader discover the many faces of masters swimming, from fitness swimmer to retired champion. Besides interesting facts and figures, it includes elements of work-outs for conditioning, strength training, and the right technique. It also features lots of tips on equipment and avoiding injury. The book is directed at every masters swimmer, with tips on finding a team, but also at coaches, with valuable help for structuring and leading a team.

200 pages, full-color print
65 photos, 47 illustrations
Paperback, 6^1/2" x 9^1/4"
ISBN: 9781841261850
$ 16.95 US / $ 29.95 AUS
£ 12.95 UK/€ 16.95

For more books on swimming visit www.m-m-sports.com

■ online
www.m-m-sports.com

■ E-Mail
sales@m-m-sports.com

■ Telephone / Fax
+49 2 41 - 9 58 10 - 13
+49 2 41 - 9 58 10 - 10

■ Mail
MEYER & MEYER Verlag
Von-Coels-Str. 390
52080 Aachen
Germany